Editor: GARY GROTH
Designer: EMORY LIU
Production: PAUL BARESH
Associate Publisher: ERIC REYNOLDS
Publishers: GARY GROTH and KIM THOMPSON

Fantagraphics Books, Inc.
7563 Lake City Way NE
Seattle WA 98115

To receive a free catalogue of more books like this, as well as an amazing variety of cutting-edge graphic novels, classic comic book and newspaper strip collections, eclectic prose novels, visually stunning art books, and uniquely insightful cultural criticism, call (800) 657-1100 or visit Fantagraphics.com. Follow us on Twitter at @fantagraphics and on Facebook at facebook.com/fantagraphics.

Special thanks to Sam Chattin, Conrad Groth, Ben Horak, Kara Krewer, Janice Lee, Ao Meng, Jason T. Miles, Anna Pederson, Madisen Semet and Kristy Valenti for editorial assistance.

Distributed in the U.S. by W.W. Norton and Company, Inc. (800) 233-4830
Distributed in Canada by Canadian Manda Group (800) 452-6642 x862
Distributed in the U.K. by Turnaround Distribution (44 (0)20 8829-3002)
Distributed to comic book stores by Diamond Comics Distributors (800) 452-6642 x215

First Fantagraphics Books edition: September 2012
ISBN 978-1-60699-538-9
Printed in Hong Kong

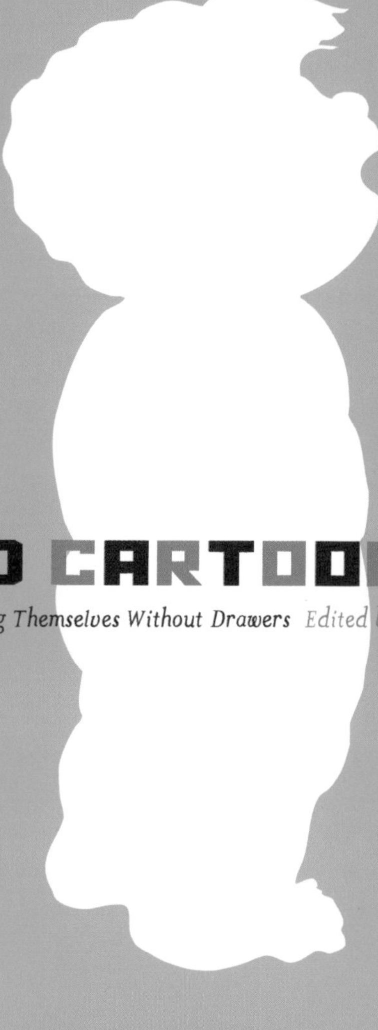

NAKED CARTOONISTS

Drawers Drawing Themselves Without Drawers Edited by Gary Groth

The nude self-caricatures of cartoonists within these pages represent the final collection my late husband, Mark J. Cohen, pursued through the last two years of his life.

At age 14 in 1956, Mark began collecting cartoonist's self-caricatures and the collection grew to approximately 400 pieces. In 1998 Ohio State University Libraries published *A Gallery of Rogues*, a wonderful assortment of 143 cartoonist's self-portraits.

Mark was a cartoon collector, historian, writer, and promoter and once was introduced as the "cartoonist's best friend" during a television interview. While cartoons were his passion, Mark was no artist and could not draw (with the exception of his own self-caricature).

The genesis of the nude collection began during a long flight home from the triennial Cartoon Art Festival at Ohio State University. During the flight, Mark and I had a hilarious conversation centered on asking our "cartoonist family" for their nude self-caricatures. The idea was to gather a dozen or more caricatures and submit them for publication in *Playboy* magazine. Lynn Johnston was the first to respond and her rendering was to be the centerfold. Mark proceeded to send Lynn's drawing to other cartoonists as inspiration, and soon we had a grand collection of over 100 pieces.

As the collection grew, Mark conceived a gallery show to display the self-caricatures. Thanks to our good friend Dan Lienau, the collection was exhibited on December 3, 1999 at the Annex Gallery in Santa Rosa, California. During this time Mark battled cancer and though his health deteriorated, he looked forward to the show opening. He arrived for his final exhibition in a wheel chair. Proud of this production which displayed his cartoonist family in such a unique way, he could now prepare for his final journey. Mark died on December 19, 1999 at home surrounded by his family and the cartoons he so loved.

Heartfelt thanks go to Jean Schulz for her encouragement and championing of this book, to Lucy Shelton Caswell for her immeasurable help with permissions, and to Gary Groth for agreeing to publish this collection. Finally, to all the cartoonists who contributed caricatures and added substance to Mark's life, a grand THANK YOU! And as Mark would say, "ENJOY!"

Rose Marie McDaniel IV

THE LONG AND SHORT OF IT

by Frank Stack

The nude has a long tradition throughout art history, and life drawing is — or ought to be — a part of virtually every artist's study. Here we present the nude self-portrait combined with the cartoonists' sly, wicked, and self-deprecating wit.

Cartoonists encounter a barrier when it comes to drawing people without clothing. The publications they draw for generally consider nudity to be forbidden. They're rigid about that.

So, given the assignment, the game becomes: How do I get away with this and how can I make it funny? Funny to whom? Since these cartoons were done at the special request of collector Mark Cohen, they may have felt less restraint than they would have if they'd tackled such an assignment from one of their commercial clients. This gave them greater latitude to tackle the basic themes of sexual vanity, misrepresentation, and manipulation, which greater liberty, in my opinion, they took advantage of with creative aplomb. In this book, of course, with one exception, they are all self-portraits, sometimes even recognizable.

Several of the cartoons in this volume deal with the futility of maintaining the illusion of personal attractiveness despite the passing years. Trina Robbins and Ann Telnaes peek from behind painted body cutouts. Lynn Johnston's parody of a centerfold pin-up is particularly poignant, reminding us that this graceful and beautiful woman caricatures herself daily as a plain person in her *For Better or For Worse* strip. Charles Schulz and Mort Walker show themselves in athletic pursuits.

There are jokes about the artists being artists, as with Wiley Miller and Jim Borgman both with accompanying pencil sharpener gags, and Arnold Roth's virtuoso foreshortening ploy. Several of the cartoonists represent themselves on stage as sleazy performers.

Others invoke the theme of the nude in art history, such as Creig Flessel's "naked" versus "nude" gag and the satyr and nymph references in Eldon Dedini's and Lee Lorenz's beautiful little paintings. Russ Myers does a turn on historical legend, presenting himself as Lord Godiva. Naturally we get some tongue-in-cheek mooning jokes, with Dan Piraro's tattooed tookus and Harley L. Schwadron's editor joke, as well as a take off on Duchamps' "Nude Descending a Staircase."

A couple of the cartoons made me laugh out loud: Will Eisner clothing himself with items found in the trash can from an inner city tenement and George Booth's self-portrait as a hair-covered primitive anthropoid.

One artist tries to avoid representing himself by offering up his most famous character instead. When Charles Schulz draws Charlie Brown being knocked off the pitcher's mound and losing all his clothes (in a variation on a classic *Peanuts* theme), he thereby reveals what everyone has long suspected — Charlie Brown has always been a self-portrait.

These cartoons stand on their own, whether one knows the cartoonists or not.

TABLE OF CONTENTS

Scott Adams (b. 1957, Windham, NY) is the creator of *Dilbert*, a comic strip that made its first appearance in April 1989. It is currently syndicated in over 2,000 newspapers in 75 countries and 25 languages, and has inspired a television show, several spin-off books and a computer game. Adams has an M.B.A from University of California, Berkeley, and has written several best-selling books on business philosophy. Adams has won the National Cartoonists Society Reuben Award and Newspaper Comic Strip Award in 1997 for his work on *Dilbert*.

He's BUCK NAKED!
Scott Adams

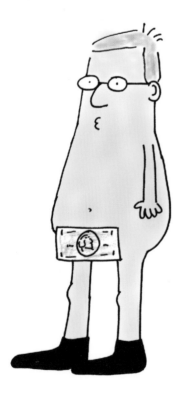

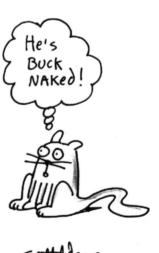

Brent E. Anderson (b. 1955, San Jose, CA)'s professional cartooning career began with his contributions to indie comics such as *Venture* in 1976. He then worked on the series *Ka-zar the Savage*, written by Bruce Jones in 1979. His next project was the X-Men graphic novel *God Loves, Man Kills*, after which he had runs on titles such as *Somerset Holmes*, *Strikeforce Morituri*, *Spinworld*, *Spider-Man*, *Gen13*, *Avengers*, *Rising Stars* and many more. He is best known for co-creating *Astro City* with Kurt Busiek, and has won several Eisner and Harvey Awards and an Inkpot Award, among other honors and recognitions. Anderson lives in Northern California with his wife and son.

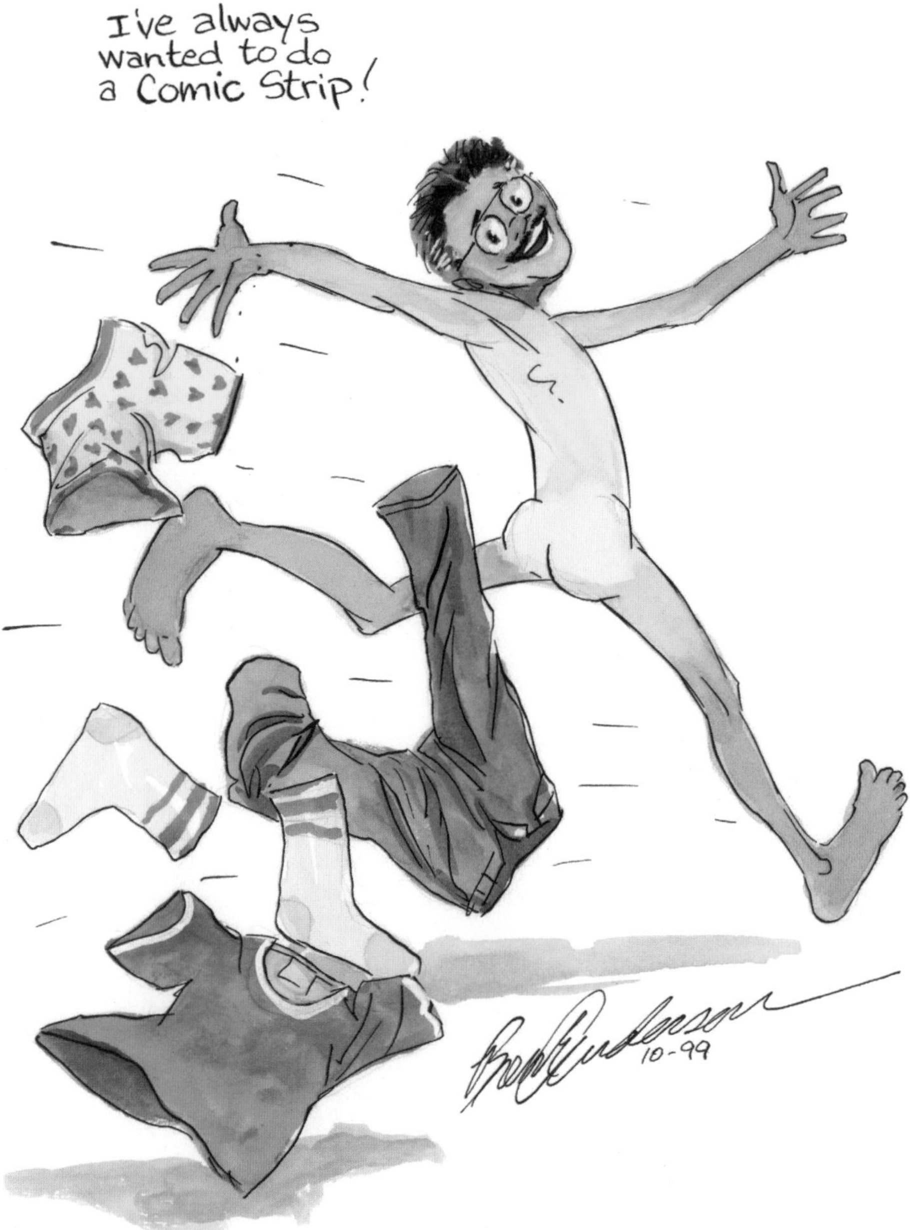
I've always
wanted to do
a Comic Strip!
10-99

Sergio Aragonés (b. 1937, San Mateu, Spain) moved with his parents to Mexico City in the wake of the Spanish Civil War, where he grew up drawing comics for his friends. He made his first professional sale in 1954 when a high school classmate submitted his work to *Ja Ja*, a humor magazine. Aragonés is best known as a *Mad* magazine cartoonist (his work has appeared in over 450 issues) and for his *Groo the Wanderer* comic book. (He's also worked as a clown and pantomime artist, mentored by Alejandro Jodorowsky.) Aragonés has won multiple awards for his work, including nine Harvey Awards, eight National Cartoonists Society Awards, and has had an award named in his honor: The Sergio, granted by the Comic Art Professionals Society. He settled in Ojai, CA.

TO MARK
MAD-LY!
ARAGONÉS

Bill Lee's response to Sergio Aragonés

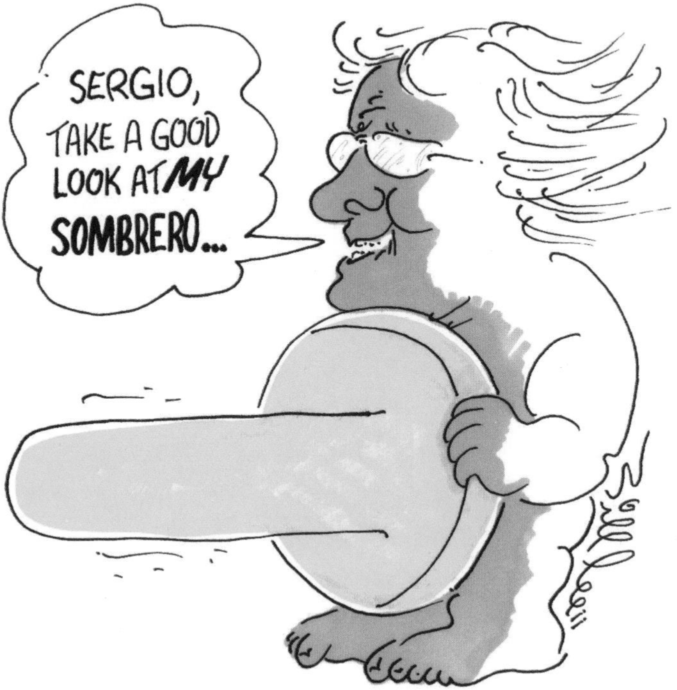
SERGIO, TAKE A GOOD LOOK AT MY SOMBRERO...

Robb Armstrong (b. 1962, West Philadelphia, PA) attended Syracuse University, graduating with a B.A. in Fine Arts. Armstrong got his break with a strip originally called *From the Hipp*, renamed *Jump Start* by the United Media syndicate. The strip borrows heavily from Armstrong's childhood and his view of the average black family. Armstrong draws the strip weekly, and does community outreach at schools. He currently lives in Pasadena with his wife Crystal.

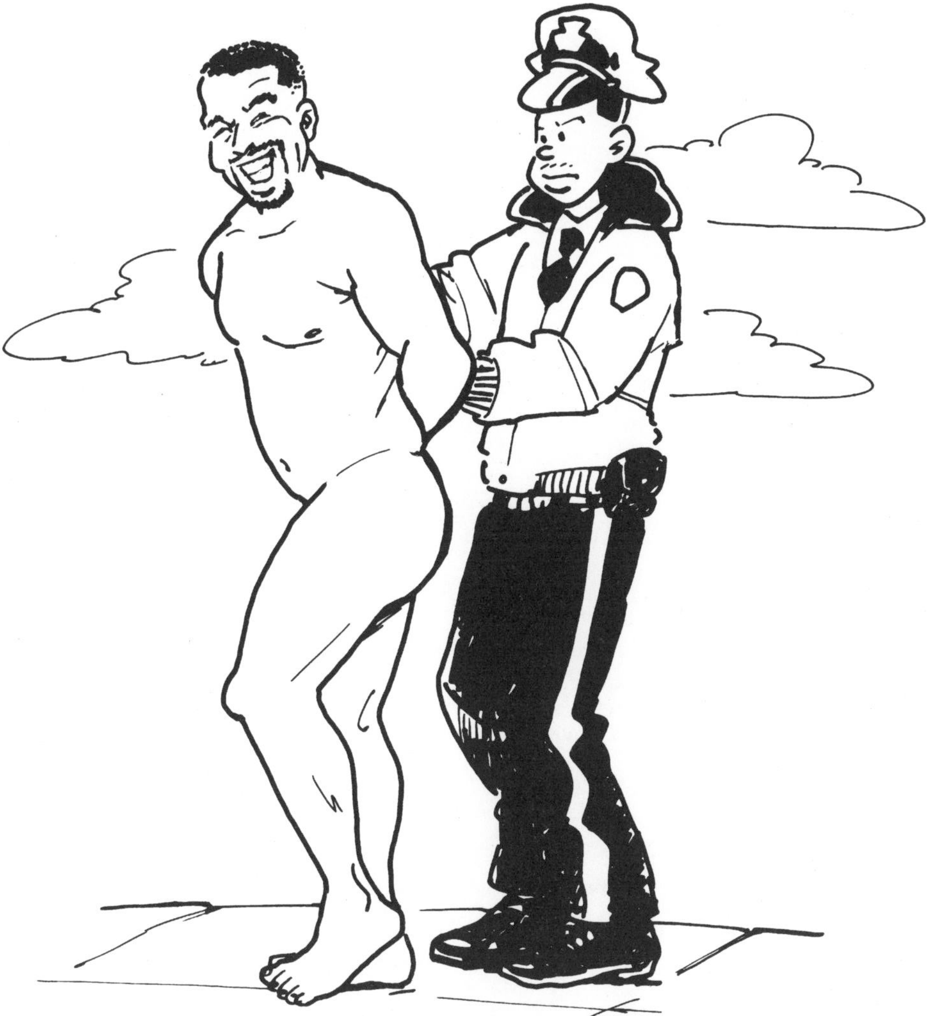
ARMSTRONG

Tom Batiuk (b. 1947, Akron, OH) is best known for his syndicated newspaper strips *Funky Winkerbean*, *John Darling*, and *Crankshaft*. Before he started drawing *Funky Winkerbean* full time, Batiuk was a junior high school teacher. He used the teaching experience to create *Funky Winkerbean*, tackling serious issues in the strip, which realistically depicted the drama of the characters as they aged. Batiuk has been nominated for a Pulitzer Prize and has won an award from the American Cancer Society for his depiction of a woman battling breast cancer. Batiuk lives with his wife and son in Medina, OH.

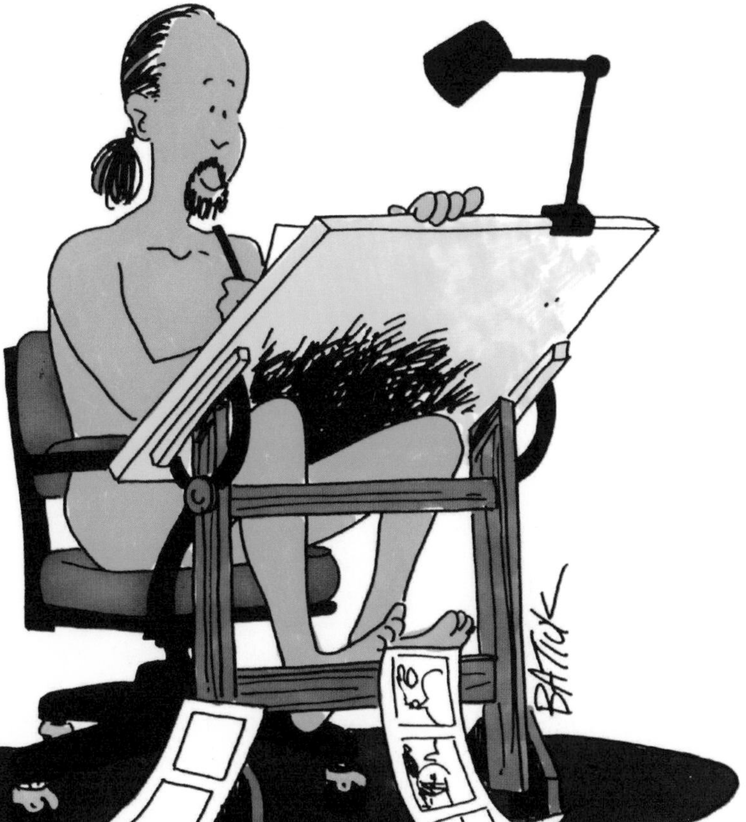
BATIUK

Chip Beck (b. 1945)'s gag, editorial and comic strip cartooning is mostly aimed at a military audience. In 1979, Beck, a veteran, got his start in *State Magazine* with his comic strip *Supercrat, The Super Bureaucrat*. Beck became the Navy's official combat artist after being sent back into active duty during Desert Storm. Later, Beck became the editorial cartoonist for *National Forum*, *Georgetown Courier*, *Sun Gazette* and *Northern Virginia Sun*. Beck also has a police-themed cartoon feature entitled *Kiljoy*. In 1996 Beck became one of the Board of Directors for The National Cartoonists Society.

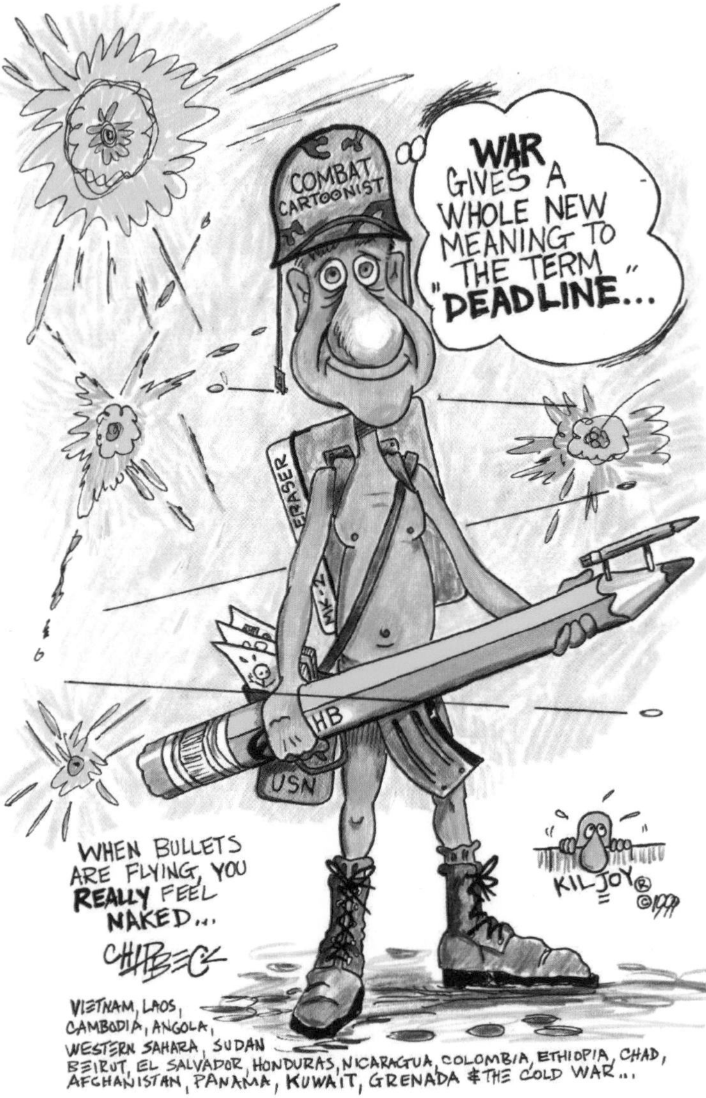
COMBAT CARTOONIST
WAR GIVES A WHOLE NEW MEANING TO THE TERM "DEADLINE..."
ERASER
MK-2
HB
USN
WHEN BULLETS ARE FLYING, YOU REALLY FEEL NAKED...
CHIP BECK
KILJOY®
©1999
VIETNAM, LAOS, CAMBODIA, ANGOLA, WESTERN SAHARA, SUDAN BEIRUT, EL SALVADOR, HONDURAS, NICARAGUA, COLOMBIA, ETHIOPIA, CHAD, AFGHANISTAN, PANAMA, KUWAIT, GRENADA & THE COLD WAR...

Stephen R. Bentley (b. 1954, Los Angeles, CA) is best known for his comic strip *Herb & Jamaal*, which has been running since 1989. Bentley has also worked as a commercial artist, and has created ads for the Los Angeles Dodgers, Wham-O Toys, the Playboy Channel and Universal Studios. He lives with his daughter in Northern California, where he is involved as a youthworker in the Episcopal Church and brews beer in his spare time.

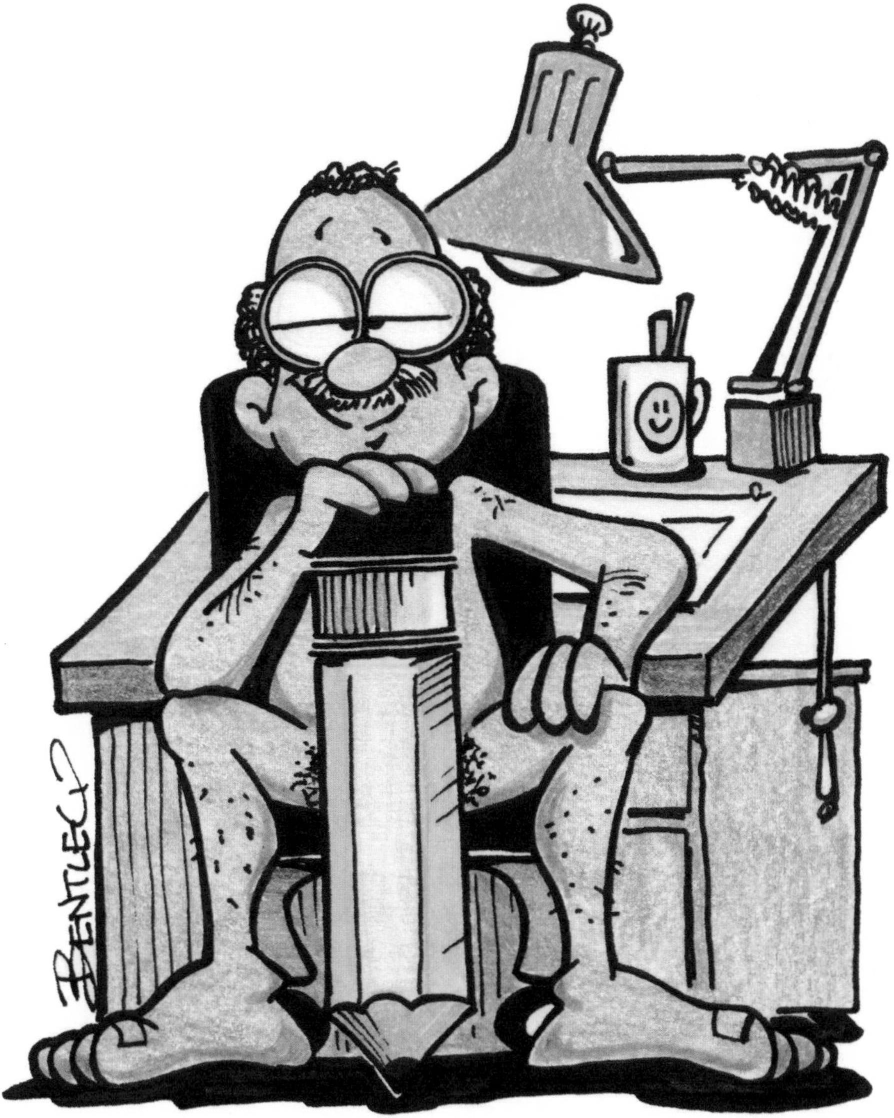
BENTLEY

George Booth (b. 1926, Cainsville, MO)'s parents were both schoolteachers, and as a result he was exposed to music, fine arts, and cartoons at an early age. Although Booth attended several art schools (The Corcoran College Of Art And Design, The Chicago Academy Of Fine Arts, The School Of Visual Arts and Adelphi College) he never graduated. In 1944, Booth was drafted into the Marine Corps. Booth was asked to re-enlist and become staff cartoonist for the Corps' *Leatherneck* magazine. Later, Booth was re-drafted for the Korean War. Booth relocated to New York, where he married and worked as a freelance artist, eventually becoming a magazine art director.

In 1956, Booth worked on the comic strip *Spot*, after which he freelanced full time, and his cartoons began running in *The New Yorker*. In 1986, Booth created a successful comic strip entitled *Local Item*. In 1993, Booth was awarded The Gag Cartoon award by The National Cartoonists Society, and in 2010, Booth received the Milton Caniff Lifetime Award. Booth resides in Stony Brook, NY.

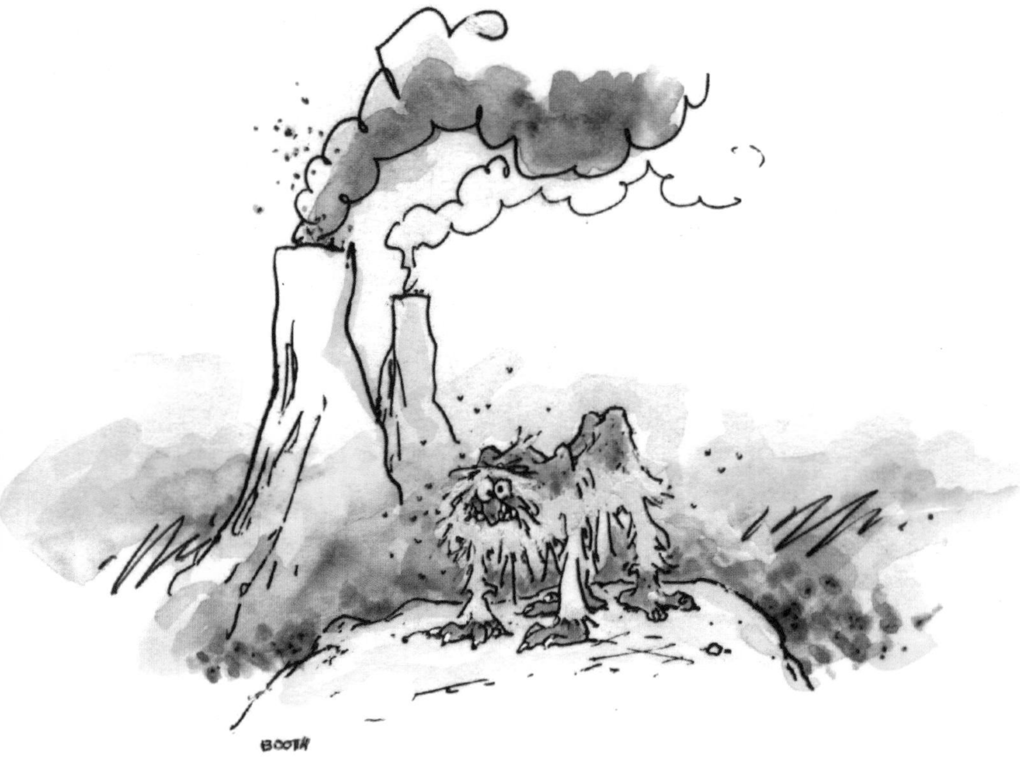
BOOTH

Jim Borgman (b. 1954, Cincinnati, OH) got his start drawing editorial cartoons for his college newspaper, the *Kenyon Collegian*. Borgman is both a syndicated editorial and comic strip cartoonist, and is best known for drawing *Zits*. Written by Jerry Scott, *Zits* appears in over 1,500 papers worldwide. In 1991, at the age of 37 he won the Pulitzer Prize. From 1994 to 1996 he crafted the weekly Bill Clinton-centric comic strip, *Wonk City* for *The Washington Post*. Sitting beside his Pulitzer are several National Cartoonists Society Editorial Cartoon Awards and the Reuben Award. Borgman lives in Cincinnati with his wife and children.

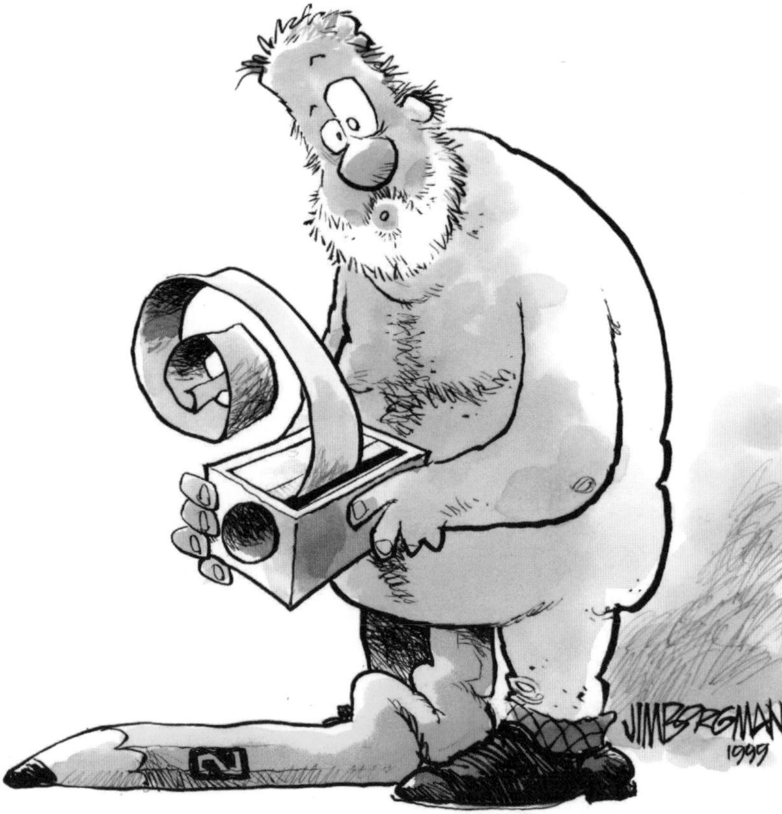
JIMBORGMAN
1999

FOR MARK and ROSIE —
PAINFULLY....
JIMBORGMAN

Paige Braddock graduated from the University of Tennessee with a degree in Fine Arts, after which she worked as an illustrator for newspapers such as *The Chicago Tribune* and *The Atlanta Constitution*. She eventually became the Creative Director at Charles M. Schulz Creative Associates, where she oversees the publication and production of licensed *Peanuts* products worldwide.

In 2002, she began self-publishing *Jane's World*, which chronicles the many humorous adventures of Jane Wyatt, lovable misfit extraordinaire. In 2006, Braddock was nominated for the Eisner Award for Best Writer/Artist in the Humor category. She currently lives with her wife in Sebastopol, CA, where she continues to create and publish *Jane's World*.

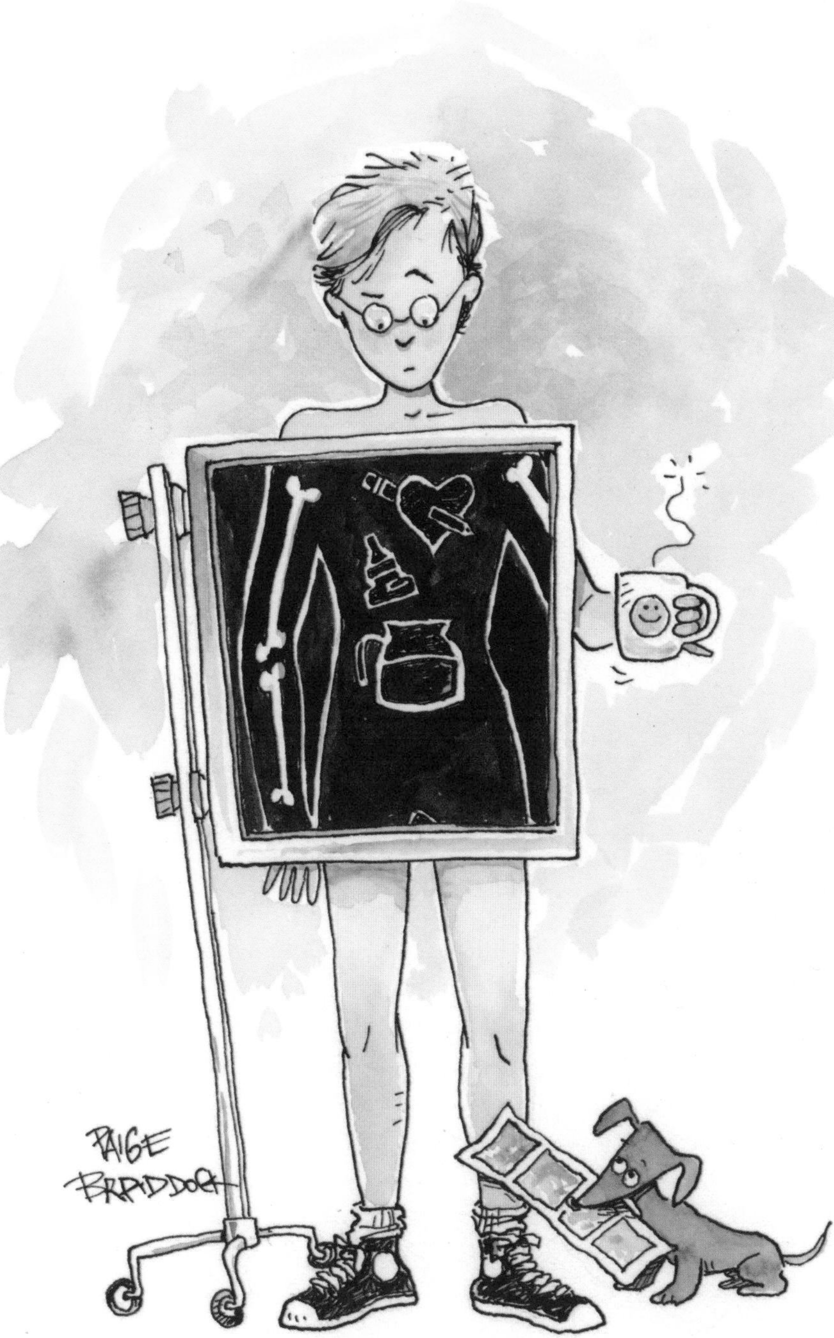
PAIGE
BRADDOCK

Robert "Buck" Brown (1936-2007, Morrison, TN) was a cartoonist, writer and painter, best known for his "Granny" character in *Playboy*. He graduated from Englewood High School, joined the United States Air Force and attended the University of Illinois. In addition to more than 600 cartoons that ran in *Playboy*, Brown has had thousands of cartoons published in *Esquire, Ebony,* and *Jet.* His paintings, which he described as "soul genre paintings," often featuring commentary on issues affecting African-Americans, were omnipresent during the Civil Rights movement. He had a son, Robert Brown, and a daughter, Lisa Hill, with his wife Mary Ellen.

to Mark Cohen from Buck Brown + granny
3/5/99

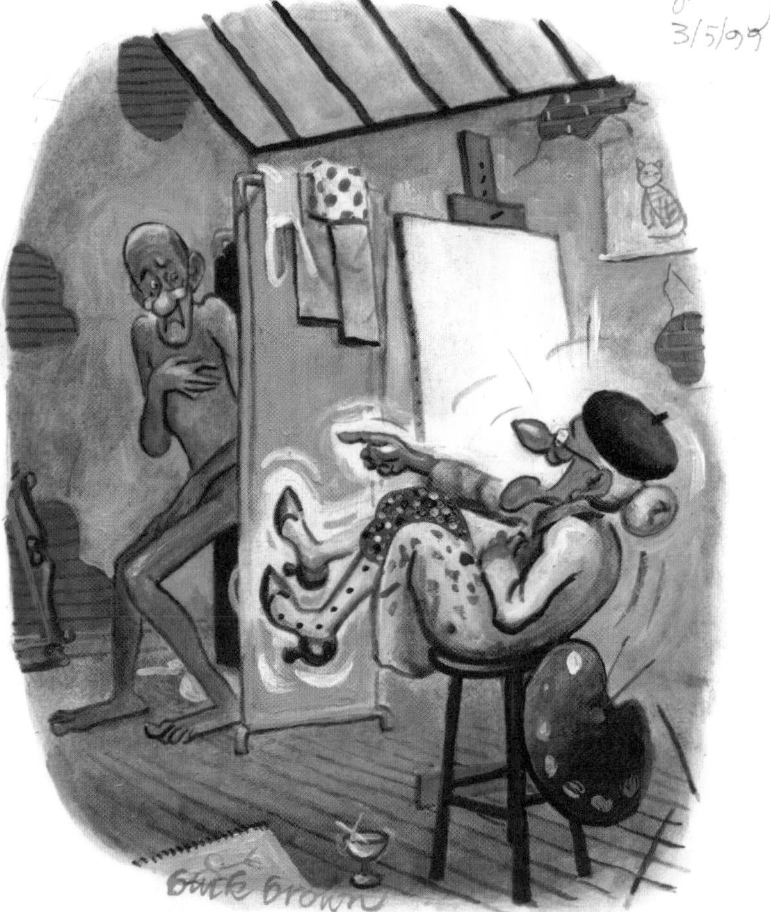
Buck Brown

Chris Browne (b. 1952, South Orange, NJ) began his career assisting his father, Dik Browne, on the comic strips *Hägar The Horrible* and *Hi And Lois*. 1985 saw the publication of *Hägar The Horrible's Very Nearly Complete Viking Handbook*, co-authored by Chris, and in 1988, after his father retired he assumed full duty on *Hägar* (which appears in over 1,900 newspapers worldwide).

In addition to his work on *Hägar,* Browne has contributed gag cartoons to *National Lampoon, Playboy, Esquire, Heavy Metal, The New Yorker* and *The National Review*. In early 2000, Chris and Carroll Browne began to write and draw a semiautobiographical comic strip, *Raising Duncan*. Browne currently resides in Sioux Falls, SD where he continues to draw *Hägar The Horrible*.

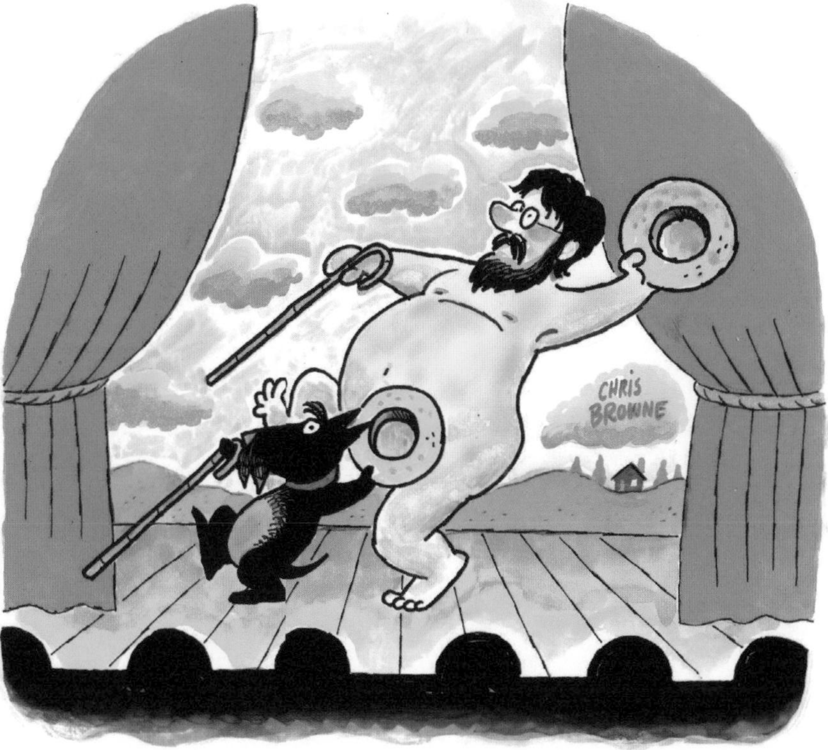
CHRIS
BROWNE

John Caldwell (b. 1946) attended the Parsons School of Design. In addition to his one-panel *Caldwell* newspaper cartoon, his work has appeared in venues such as *The New Yorker*, *Playboy*, *National Lampoon* and *Mad*. He is also the designer of many fine greeting cards. He lives with his wife in upstate New York.

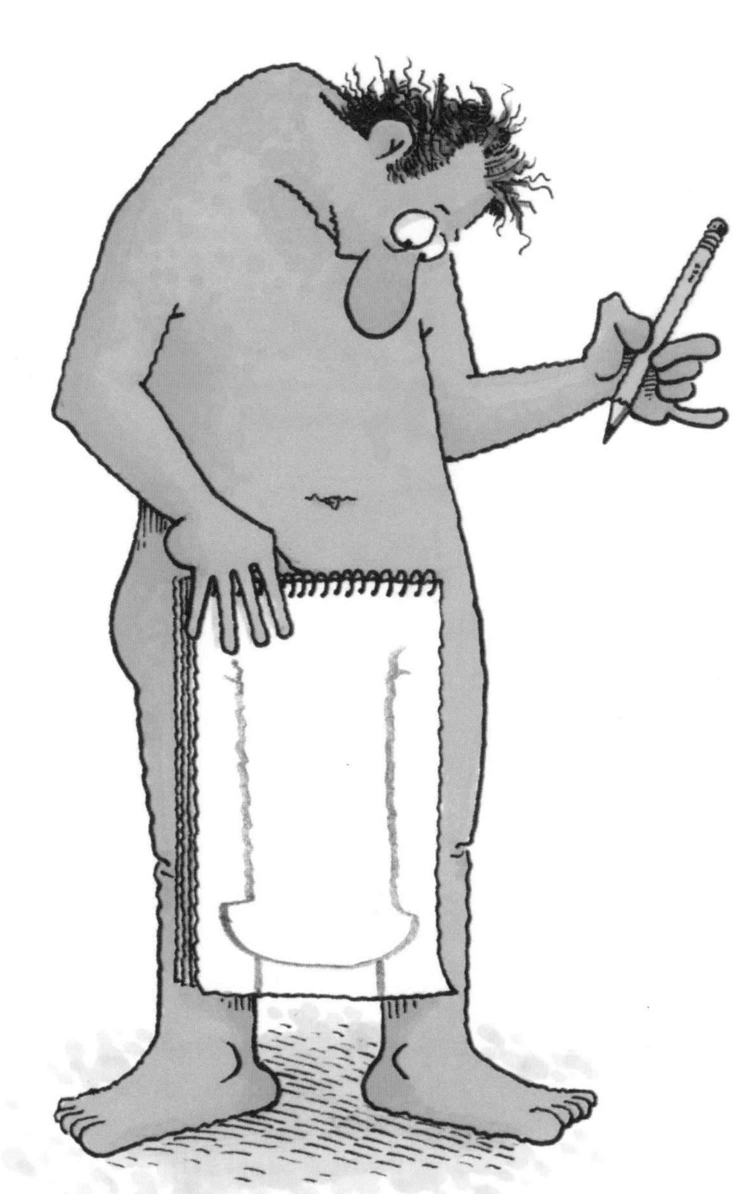
CALDWELL.....

Bob Clarke (b. 1926, Mamaroneck, NY) started his career while in high school. He was an uncredited assistant on the *Ripley's Believe It or Not* comic strip (years later he illustrated the *Mad* parody, credited), until he was drafted into the U.S. Army as a combat radioman. Upon his return, he found work at *Stars and Stripes*. 1949-1955 saw Clarke try his hand at advertising, freelance illustration and graphic design until he began his long tenure at *Mad* magazine in 1956. Clarke resides in Seaford, DE.

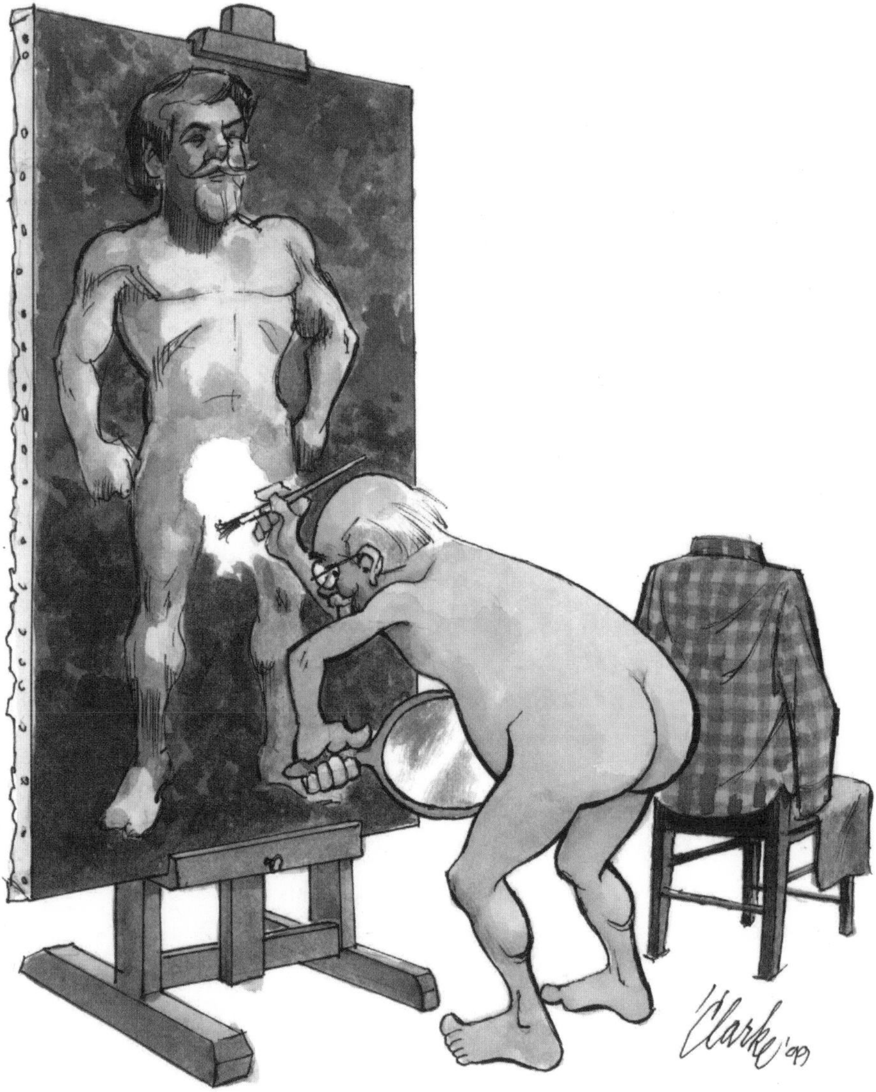
Clarke '09

Clive Collins (b. 1942, in Somerset, England) studied graphic design at the Kingston School of Art, and worked various jobs in marine insurance and film. He contributed to *Punch* magazine until he became the political and editorial cartoonist for the *Sun* in 1969, which he worked for through 1982. During that time, he also contributed gag cartoons to *The People* and *Playboy*. Since 1985, he's been *Reader's Digest* featured artist and worked with *The Sporting Life* until 1999. In 2000, his strip *Baby Blair* ran in *The Daily Mail*. He has been awarded Cartoonist of the Year by the Cartoonists' Club of Great Britain in 1984, 1985 and 1987. He is the Secretary of the British Cartoonists Association, as well as the Life Vice-President of the Cartoonists' Club of Great Britain. In 2011, he was appointed MBE (Member of the Most Excellent Order of the British Empire) for the Queen's Birthday Honors. He lives with his wife, and continues to cartoon in East England.

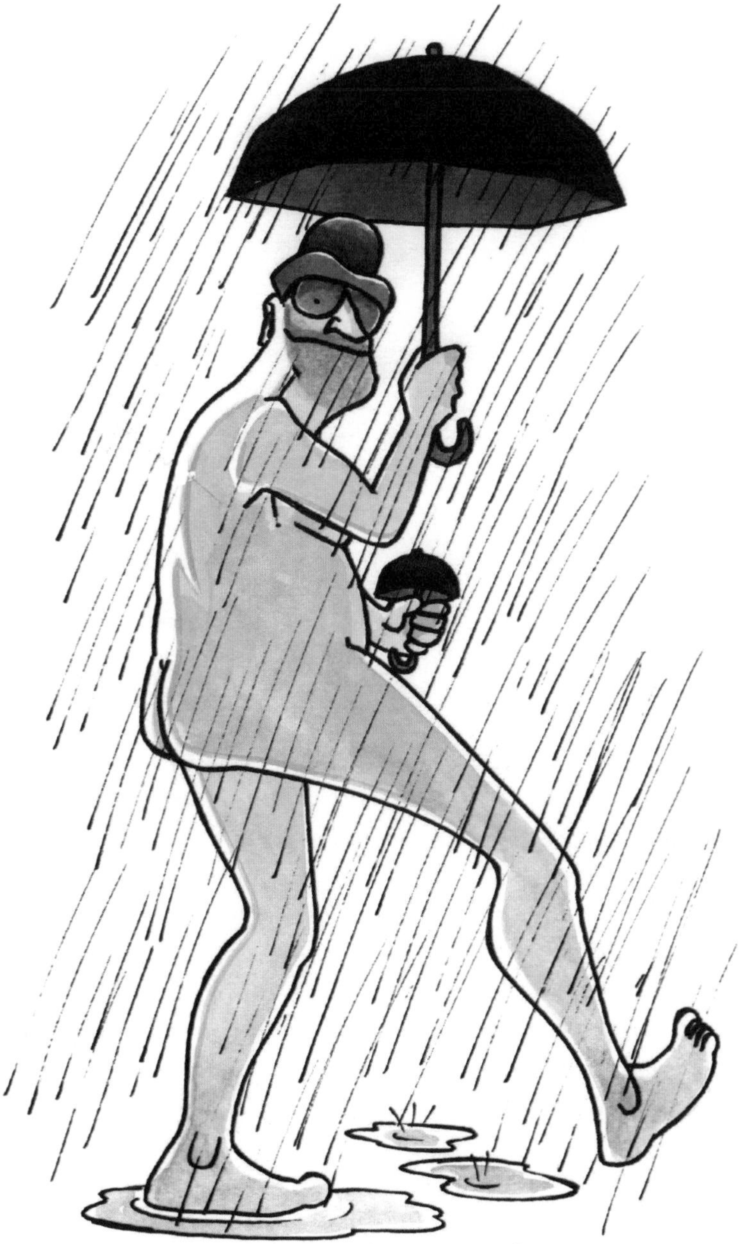

Art Cummings (b. 1922, Barre, VT)'s ambition was "to learn to draw funny and express humor." While attending Pratt Institute (class of '47) he drew cartoons for *The Saturday Evening Post* and *Collier's*. He produced covers for *American Weekly* and illustrations for *Family Circle, Woman's Day, Reader's Digest* and many more magazines. For a time, Cummings worked in a professional film think tank, and collaborated with Henny Yougman on the comic strip *Henny*. Cummings has illustrated many children's books including *The Cat's Pajamas, Septimus Bean and His Amazing Machine, There's a Monster Eating My House* and *Please Try to Remember the First of Octember!* (written by Dr. Seuss). Cummings' most recent work can be found in *Penthouse* and *Omni*.

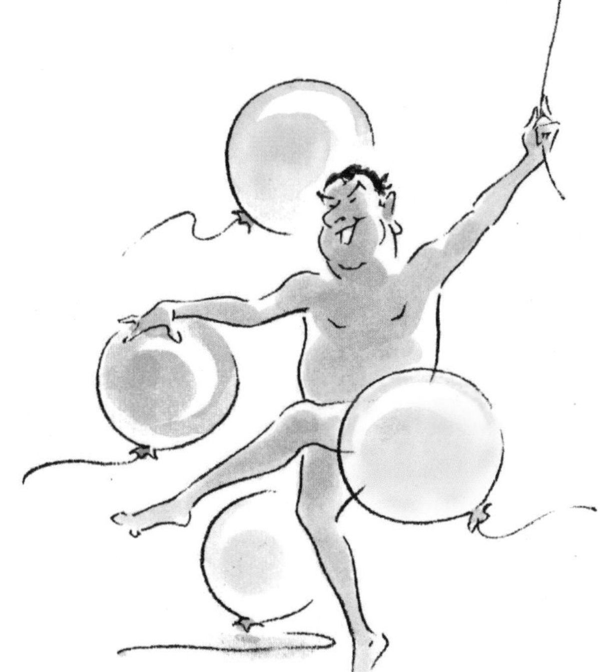
Cumings

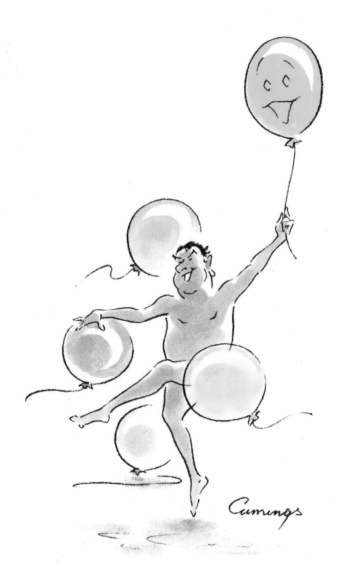

Barbara Dale is a native of Kentucky. She is a cartoonist, illustrator, and writer known for her brand of alternative greeting cards, Dale Cards. Her images have also appeared on mugs, calendars and various other gift-industry products. She is also a syndicated cartoonist (*The Stanley Family*) and authored *The Working Woman Book* and *The Joys of Motherhood*.

Dale's work had been published in the *L.A. Times*, *London Herald*, *Cosmopolitan* and *People*. In 2002 she was an award finalist in National Cartoonists Society Greeting Card Division. She lives in Baltimore, MD.

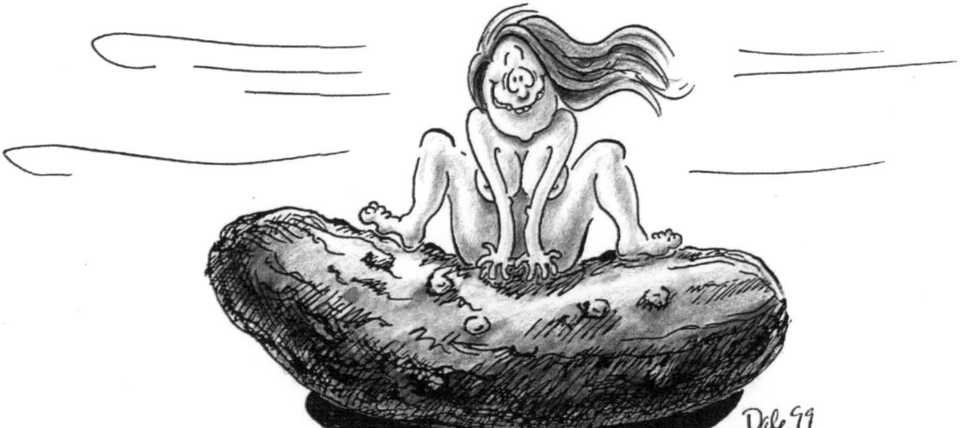
Dale 99

NUDE SELF-CARICATURE ON KOSHER DILL PICKLE IN WIND.

Eldon Dedini (1926-2006 King City, CA) mastered a variety of styles, as evidenced by the work he did for *Disney*, *Esquire*, *The New Yorker* and *Playboy*, among others. Dedini is most recognized for the many lush and sensuous watercolors he produced for *Playboy*. Lascivious and playfully erotic, his single image cartoons for *Playboy* defined the apex of men's magazine cartooning and have yet to be bested. The National Cartoonists Society granted him four of their awards in the Gag Cartoon category. His gigantic collection, *An Orgy of Playboy's Eldon Dedini* was published in 2006 (Fantagraphics Books). He settled in Carmel Valley, CA, where he died in 2006.

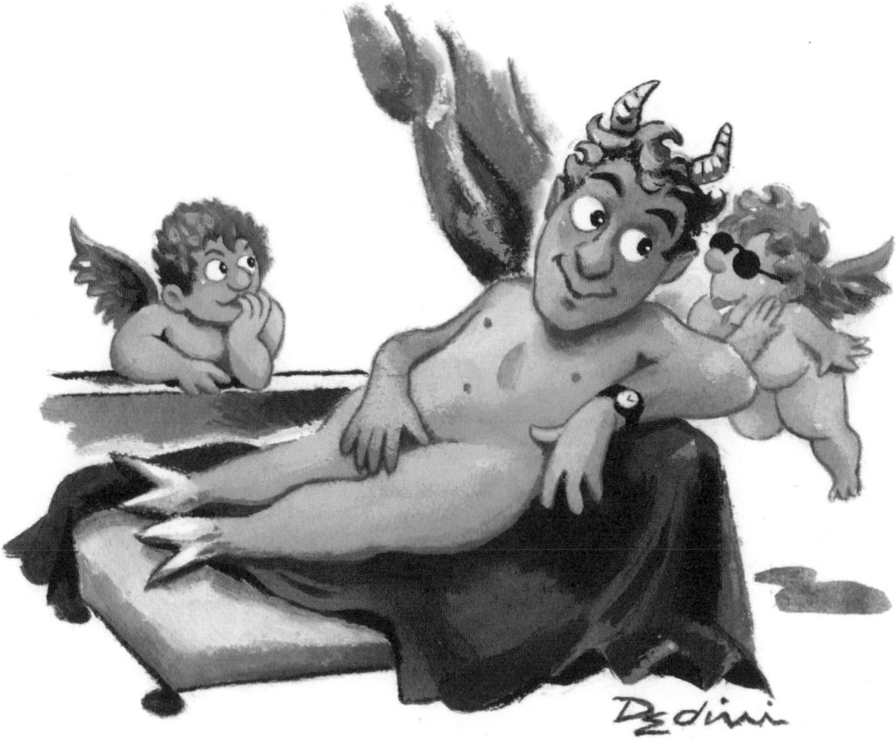
Dedini

John Dempsey (1919-2002, Sierra Madre, CA), traveled with a minor rodeo circuit and worked with horses on a ranch in Arizona, all the while keeping notebooks filled with drawings of horses and cowboys. As a Sea Bee for the Navy he was an artist, cartoonist, and art editor of the *Sea Bee Magazine*. After he finished service in 1945, he moved back to California and enrolled at Chouinard Art Institute of Los Angeles, but dropped out after two years when *Collier's* accepted a cartoon submission for $60. He soon had work in *The Saturday Evening Post, Look,* and *Cosmopolitan*. In 1954 he submitted a batch of single-panel cartoons to the new men's magazine *Playboy*. Hugh Hefner purchased one of the drawings, and Dempsey's cartoons appeared in almost every issue thereafter. He met and married his wife Ann in 1969, and moved to Del Mar where they had two children.

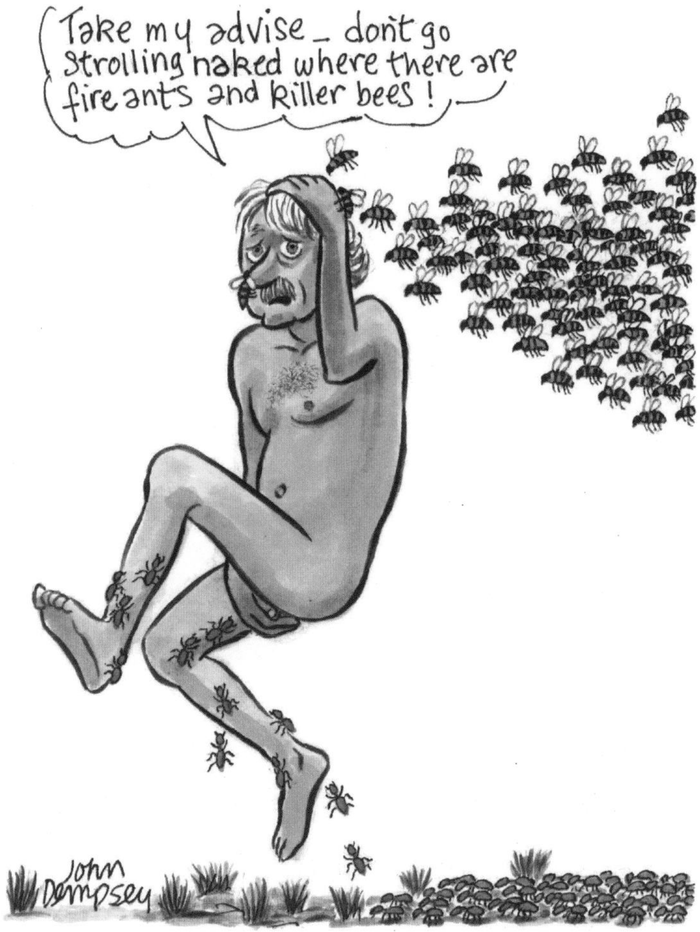
Take my advise _ don't go strolling naked where there are fire ant's and killer bees !
John Dempsey

Rick Detorie (b. 1954, Baltimore, MD) graduated with a B.F.A. from the Maryland Institute College of Art, and moved to Southern California to work as an art director for a Los Angeles ad agency, eventually making his way up to creative director. Freelancing, he did work for such magazines as *National Lampoon*, *Saturday Evening Post*, *Penthouse* and *Omni*. During the 1980s, Detorie drew *Alvin and the Chipmunks* for Bagdasarian Productions, which included storybooks, album covers and other merchandise. On Sept. 11, 1988, he had his comic strip *One Big Happy* syndicated by Creators Syndicate. The strip is still running, and has been collected into four anthologies. Detorie has also published numerous humor books, including *The Official Cat Dictionary*, *No Good Men*, *Totally Tacky Cartoons*, *How to Survive an Italian Family* and *No Good Lawyers*. He currently lives in Venice Beach, CA.

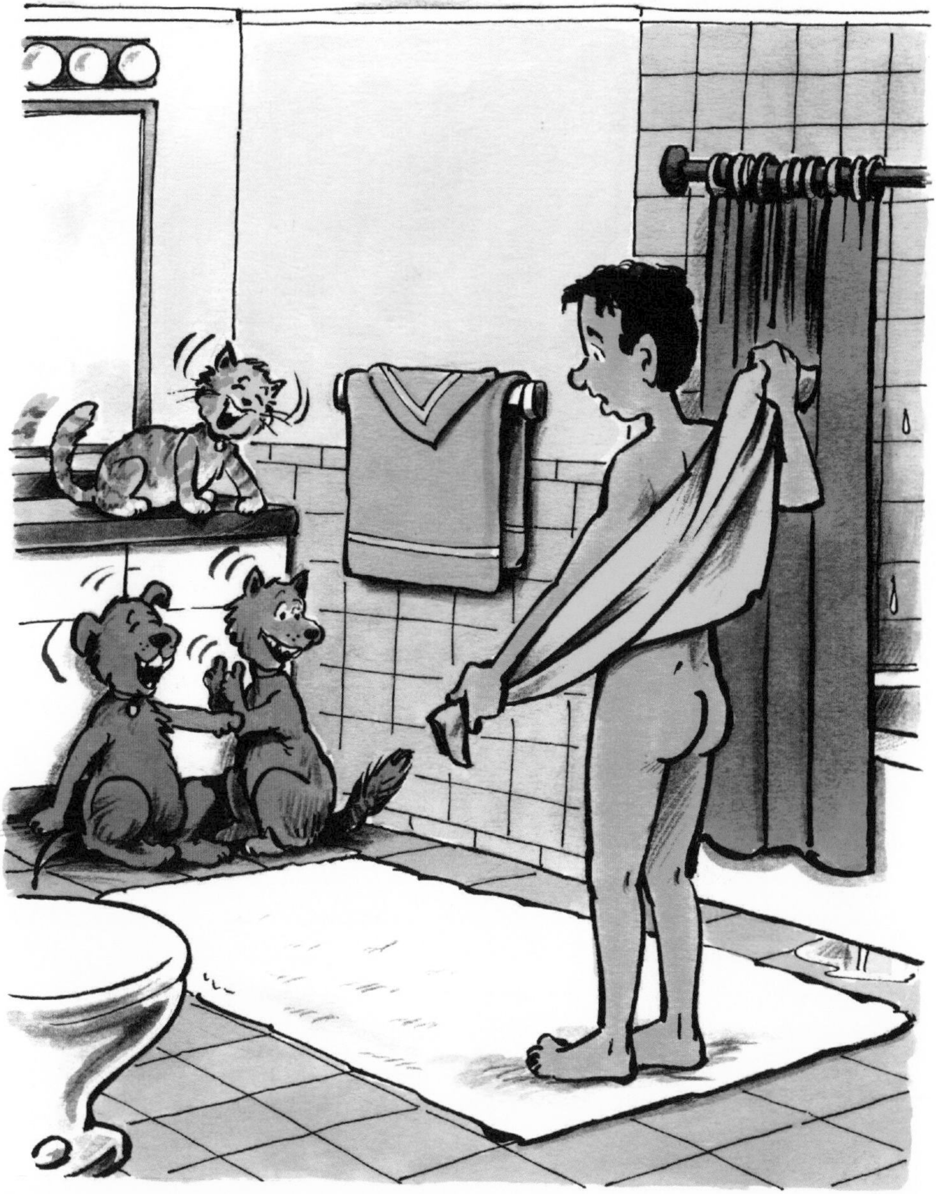

WHY ALL OF MY PETS HAVE BEEN FIXED.

RICK detorie

Hy Eisman (b. 1927) created his first newspaper cartoon feature, *It Happened in New Jersey*, in the mid-1950s, after a short stint as a greeting card artist. He then assisted the likes of Alfred Andriola and Vernon Greene, and worked on comic books such as *Adventures into the Unknown*, *Forbidden Worlds*, *Blondie*, *Nancy*, *Twilight Zone* and *Smokey Stover*. From 1967 to 1983 Eisman illustrated Jimmy Hatlo's comic series *Little Iodine*. In 1986 he took over the world's oldest comic strip, *The Katzenjammer Kids*, and in 1994 began drawing the Sunday comic strip *Popeye*. Eisman won the National Cartoonists Society's Award for Best Humor Comic Book Cartoonist for his *Nancy* comic books in 1975, and in 1984 he received similar recognition for his work on the *Little Lulu* comic book. In 1976, Eisman began teaching at the Joe Kubert School of Cartoon and Graphic Art in Glen Rock, NJ, where he currently resides with his family.

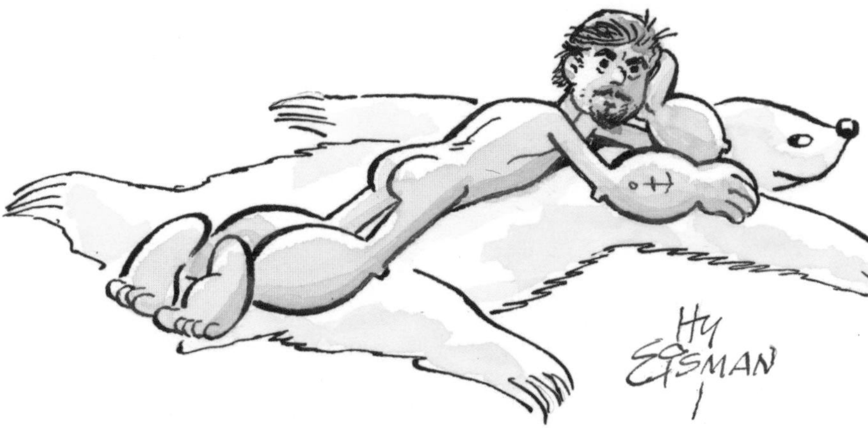
HY EISMAN

FROM POPHY ... TO MARK & ROSIE ♡♡

Will Eisner (1917-2005, Brooklyn, NY) got his start in comics in 1936 when he was published in *WOW What A Magazine!* Shortly thereafter Eisner and Jerry Iger started the Eisner-Iger Studio. After co-creating many comics, Eisner left the studio and went to work at Quality Comics Group. While there, Eisner crafted the comic he is best known for, *The Spirit*. In 1942, Eisner was drafted into the Army, and resumed his work on *The Spirit* upon his return.

Eisner was instrumental in popularizing the "graphic novel" with works such as *A Contract With God* and *The Building*, and created the educational works *Comics And Sequential Art* and *Graphic Storytelling and Visual Narrative*. Eisner was inducted into the Academy of Comic Book Arts Hall of Fame, the Jack Kirby Hall of Fame and won the Reuben Award. Named in his honor, The Will Eisner Comic Industry Awards act as the comic's industry's version of "the Oscars." Eisner passed away in 2005.

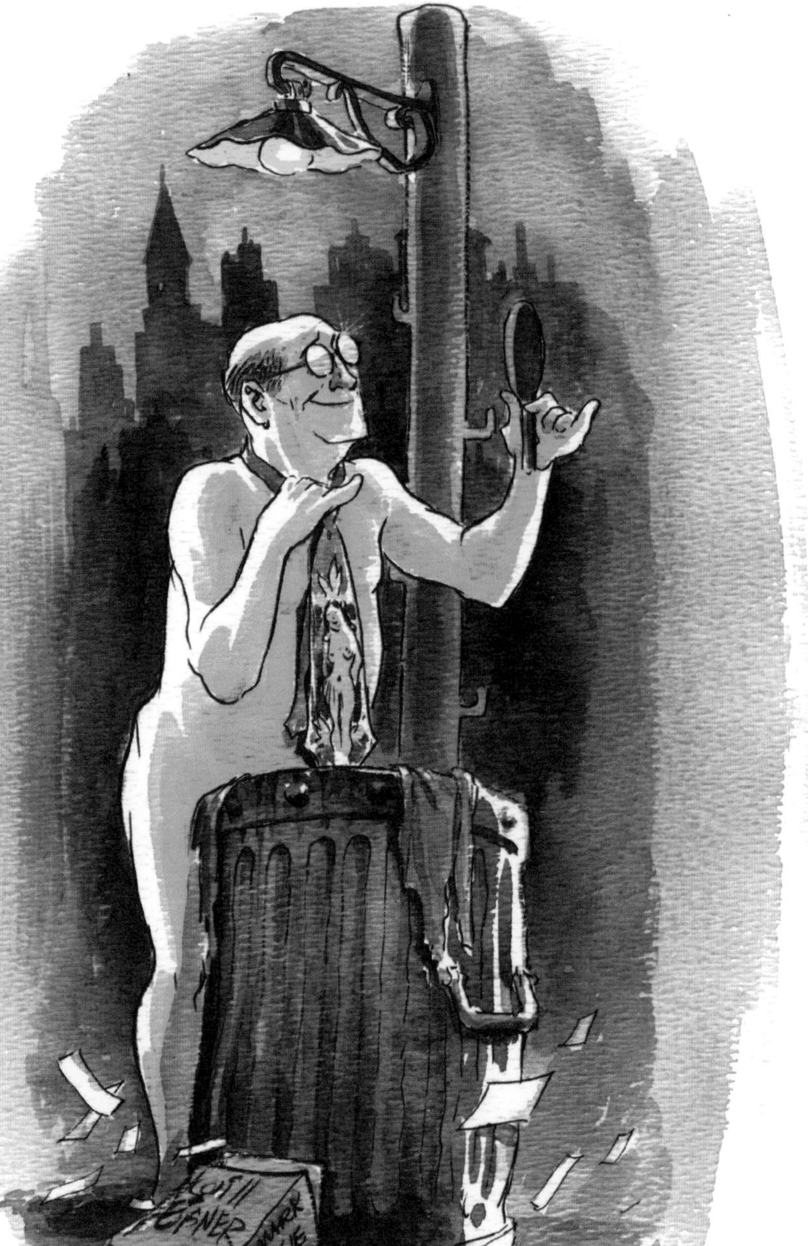
EISNER
TO MARK AND ROSIE

Will Elder (1921-2008, Bronx, NY) went to the High School of Music and Art with fellow cartoonist and future collaborator, Harvey Kurtzman. After a year of schooling at the National Academy of Design, he was drafted into the Army, where he was assigned to draw maps. Back in the States, Elder married Jean Strashun in 1948 and helped form the satirical aesthetic of *Mad* from its inception as a comic book in 1952 till 1956. He and *Mad* founder Harvey Kurtzman both left to create the humor magazines *Trump, Humbug,* and *Help!,* the latter of which featured their collaboration, *Goodman Beaver.* From 1962 to 1988, Kurtzman and Elder produced the fully painted comic *Little Annie Fanny* for Hugh Hefner's *Playboy.* Elder passed away in New Jersey on May 14, 2008.

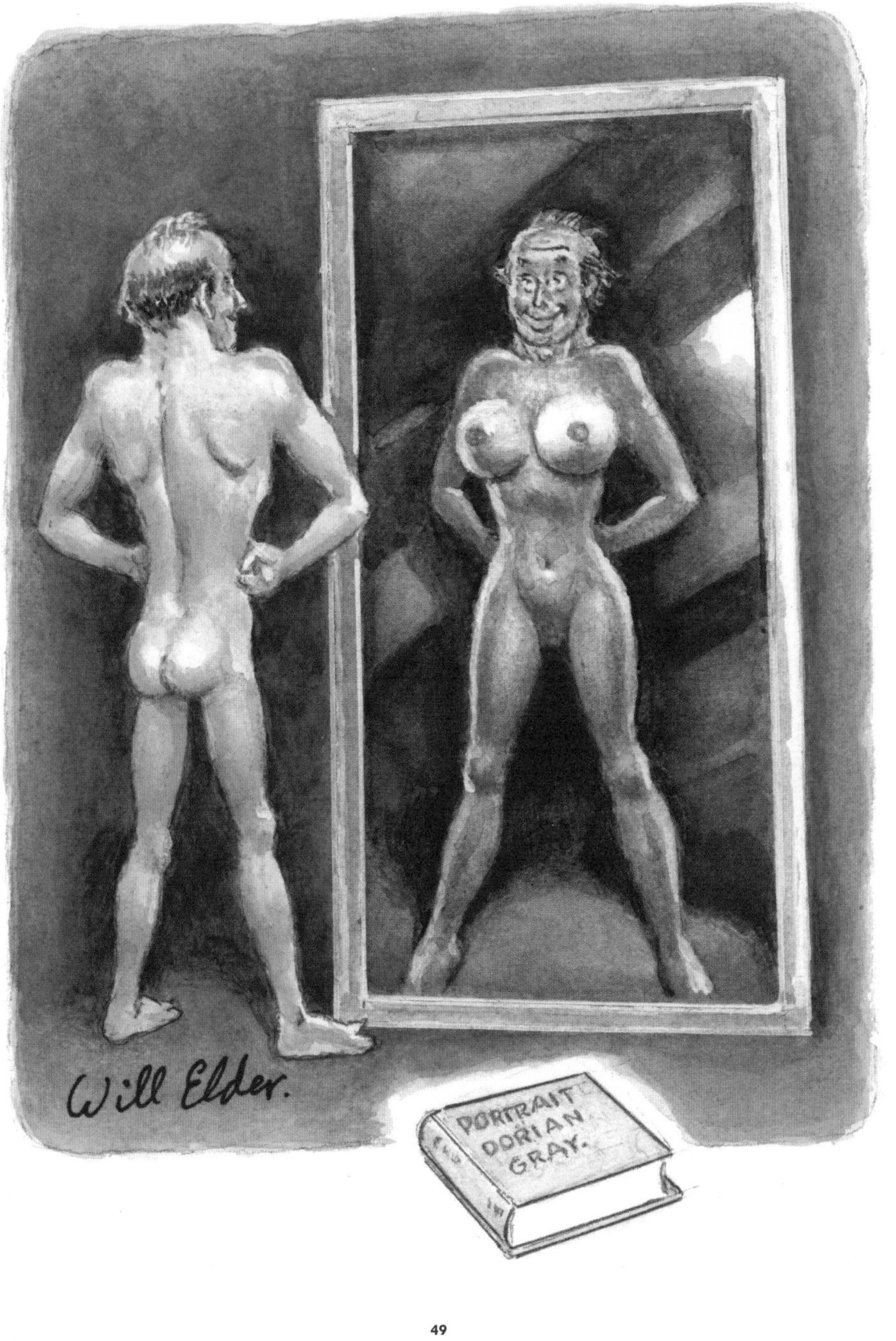
Will Elder.
PORTRAIT DORIAN GRAY.

Jan Eliot (b. 1950, San Jose, CA) was raised in the Midwest. She studied drawing, painting and ceramics at Southern Illinois University, relocating to Oregon after graduation. Her first strip, *Patience and Sarah*, ran for five years in several different publications. Soon, she began *Sister City*, which ran in *The Register-Guard* in Eugene, OR. Renamed *Stone Soup* in 1995, the strip runs in around 200 newspapers in six different countries. Eliot, who has two daughters, continues to live and work in Eugene.

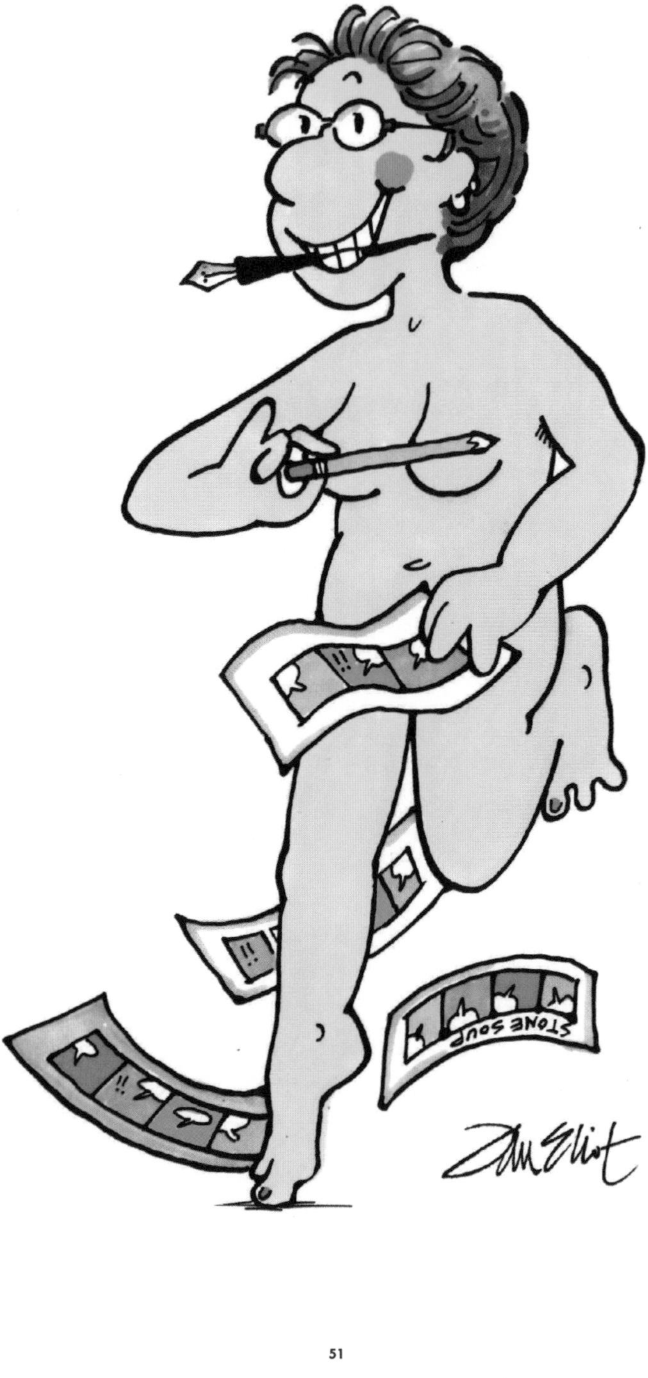
STONE SOUP

Alden Erikson (b. 1928) started working for *Playboy* in 1957. It is his work for Hugh Hefner's magazine for which he is best known. 1972 saw the publication of *Playboy's Alden Erikson*. Erikson's work has also appeared in *The Saturday Evening Post*, *The New Yorker* as well as other prestigious publications. Erikson started working in the advertising field in 1980. Erikson lives in California with his wife, Norma.

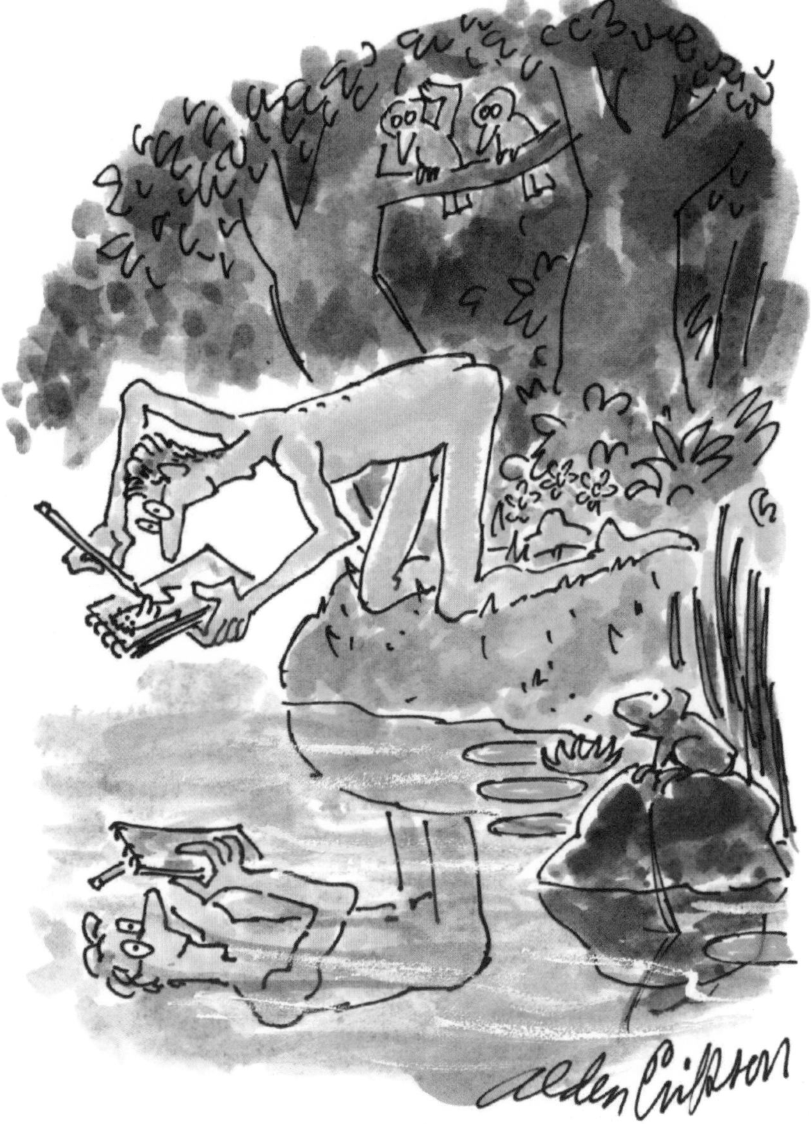

Greg Evans (b. 1947, Los Angeles, CA) grew up near Disney Studios and was influenced by comics and illustration from a very early age. A high school art teacher, he lived for a short time in Australia, eventually settling in Colorado. After a series of unsuccessful comic strips, Evans made his mark with the now well-known comic strip, *Luann*, which he sold to News America Syndicate in 1987. Prior to *Luann*, Evans created the comic strip *Fogarty* and distributed it to local high school newspapers for free. Evans received the 2003 National Cartoonists Society Reuben Award for *Luann*. He wrote and staged a musical in 2008 based on his comic strip called *Luann: Scenes in a Teen's Life*. He currently lives with his wife Betty in San Marcos, CA.

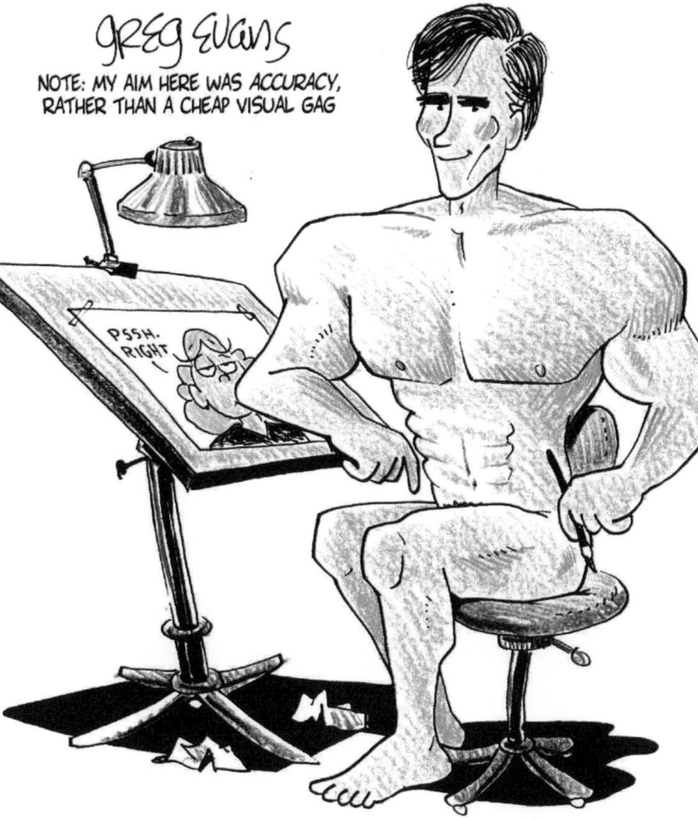
GREG EVANS
NOTE: MY AIM HERE WAS ACCURACY, RATHER THAN A CHEAP VISUAL GAG
PSSH. RIGHT

TO MARK N' ROSIE - WITH NAKED AFFECTION,
GREG EVANS

Jules Feiffer (b. 1929, Bronx, NY) is a cartoonist, author, playwright, and screenwriter. He attended James Monroe High School, and at age 16 assisted Will Eisner on the weekly seven-page strip *The Spirit*. Feiffer's strip *Sick Sick Sick,* which earned him a Pulitzer Prize, began in 1956 and ran in *The Village Voice* for 42 years. He also wrote two novels and several children's books, including *A Barrel Full of Laughs and A Vale Full of Tears*. Additionally, Feiffer wrote numerous plays, including *Little Murders* (1971), and screenplays, including *Carnal Knowledge* (1971). In 1961 he received a George Polk award for his cartooning, and an Academy Award in animated shorts for *Munro*. Feiffer was elected to the American Academy for Arts and Letters in 1995, and in 2004 received the National Cartoonists Society's Milton Caniff Lifetime Achievement Award.

you No yes No yes
No I said
no, yes
you
do yes
No I
really
mean
it No yes
No yes
No yes No
yes No yes
No No yes
yes No yes
yes No All
you
think
of
is
one
thing

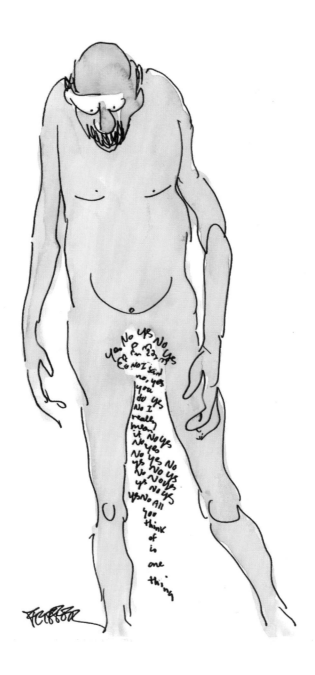

Paul H. Fell was raised in Massachusetts, but moved to Nebraska to attend college, study art and play football. While in Nebraska, he met his future wife Arlene and began to pursue a career in cartooning. He began his career as a high school art teacher and a coach, and spent several years as an art professor at Peru State College. He was an editorial cartoonist for the *Lincoln Journal* from 1984 to 1992. Since then, he has been operating his own freelance business, Paul Fell Studios. He continues to create a weekly editorial cartoon for the Nebraska Press Association and draw cartoons for the *Huskers Illustrated Magazine*. In 2005, Artizans Syndicate began distributing Fell's cartoons to newspapers worldwide.

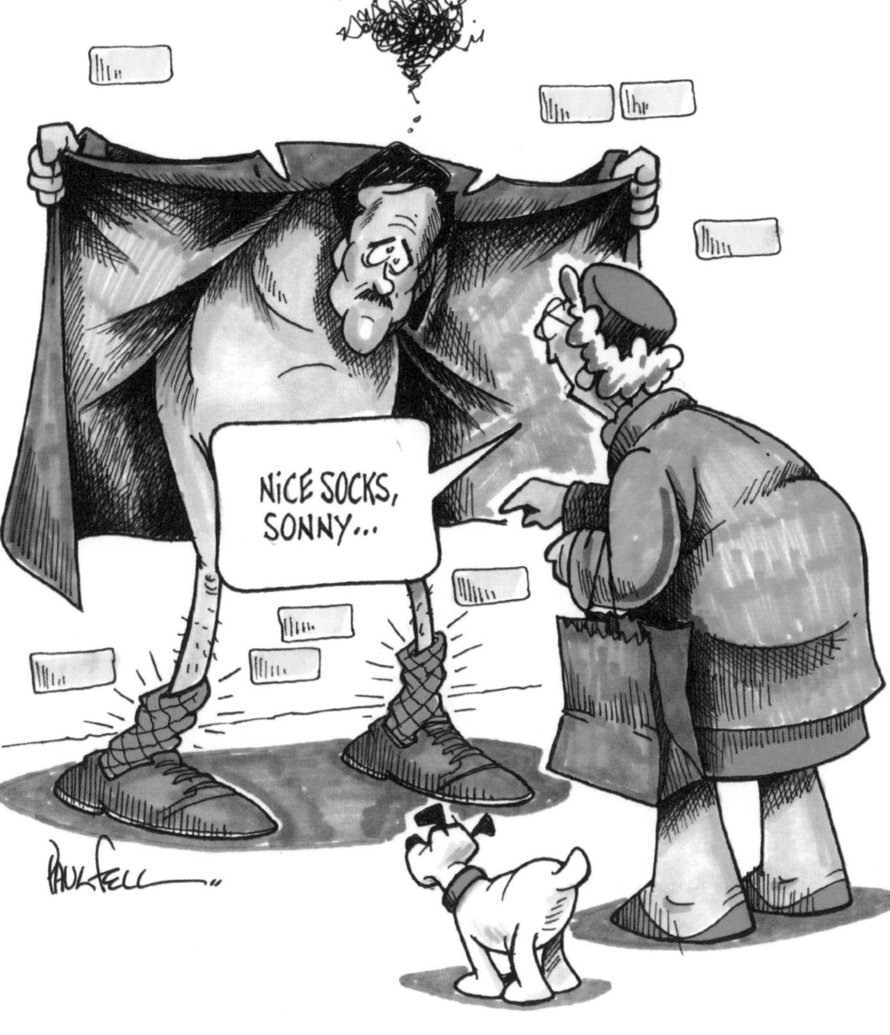
NiCE SOCKS,
SONNY...

Creig Flessel (1912-2008, Huntington, NY) attended the Grand Central Art School in New York, before starting his career as an assistant to John Streibel on the newspaper strip *Dixie Dugan*. While working on *Dixie Dugan*, Flessel also produced popular advertising art for the prominent Johnstone and Cushing agency.

Flessel is best known as one of the original DC comic artists. From the earliest issues of *Detective Comics*, Flessel illustrated the majority of the early covers. Flessel also worked on comics such as the original Sandman and The Shining Knight for *Adventure Comics*. Flessel is credited as the co-creator of *Speed Saunders*, *Hank The Cowhand*, *The Bradley Boys* and *Pep Morgan*. He followed editor Vin Sullivan to Columbia Comics, and became associate editor at Magazine Enterprises. In the 1950s, Flessel returned to DC and worked as an inker for Superman-related titles. Between 1960 and 1971 Flessel occasionally assisted Al Capp on *Lil' Abner*. In 1960 Flessel took over *David Crane* from Win Mortimer. Flessel continued to create comics well into the 1980s with the strip *Tales Of Baron Von Furstinbed* for *Playboy*. Flessel passed away in July of 2008.

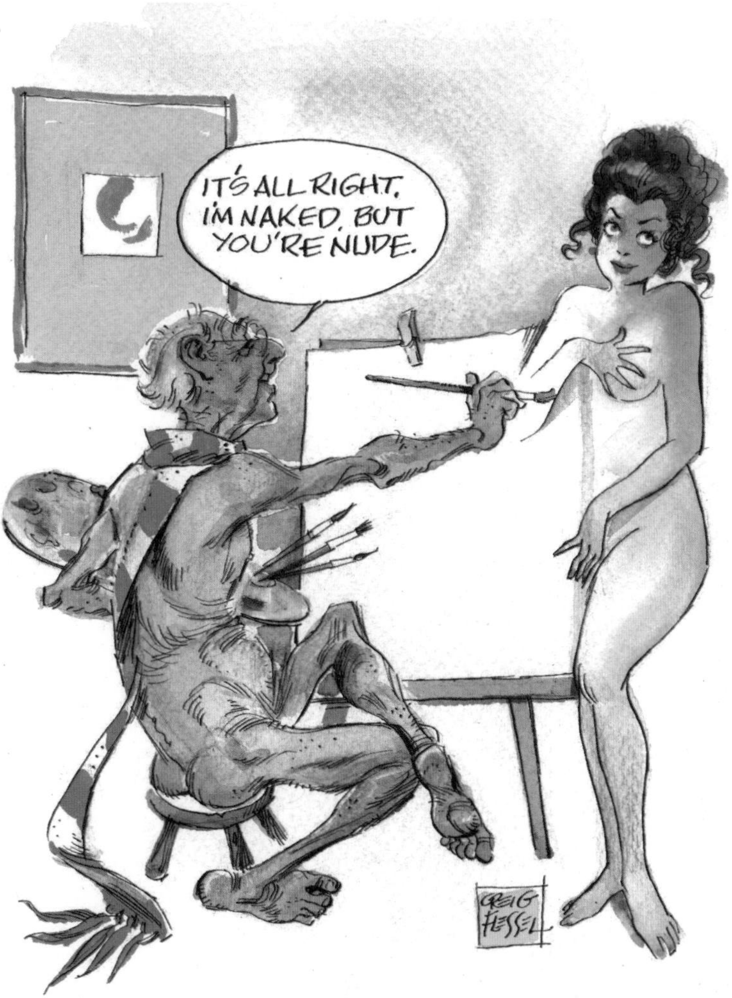
IT'S ALL RIGHT. I'M NAKED, BUT YOU'RE NUDE.
GREIG FLESSEL

Frank Kelly Freas (1922-2005, Hornell, NY) was trained in art by the influential Elizabeth Weiffenbach at Lafayette High School in Buffalo, NY. He entered the Army Air Forces after high school, and painted bomber noses during WWII. After the war, he studied at the Art Institute of Pittsburgh and began working in advertising. In 1950, Freas did his first fantasy magazine cover, illustrating H. Russell Wakefield's short story "The Third Shadow." He married Pauline Bussardin in 1952 and they had two children. He continued to do covers for fantasy and science fiction magazines, such as *Astounding Science Fiction*, and he painted many *Mad* covers from 1958-1962. His art was featured on innumerable fantasy/sci-fi paperback covers for publishers such as DAW, Signet, Ballantine, Avon and Ace Books. In addition to his fantasy/sci-fi work, he painted the insignia design for NASA's Skylab I, over 500 portraits of saints for the Franciscans, and the album art for Queen's *News of the World*. He leaves a wife Laura in California.

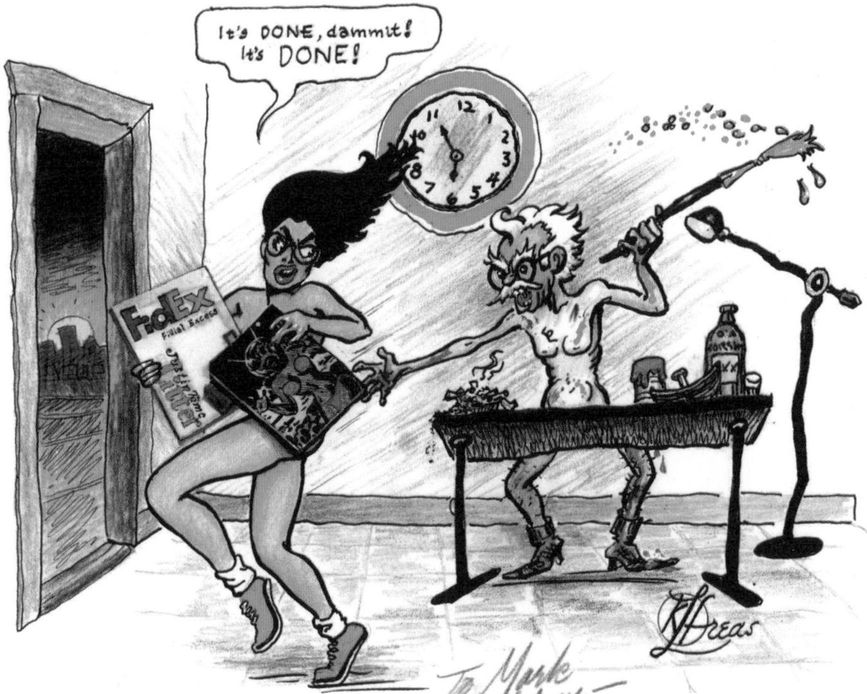
It's DONE, dammit! It's DONE!
FidEx
Filial Excess
To Mark
with love—

Bill Gallo (1922-2011, NY) worked as a copy boy at the *Daily News* after graduating from high school. Shortly thereafter, he joined the Marines to serve in WWII, where he saw action at Iwo Jima. When he returned, he continued to work at the *Daily News* as a caption writer, layout artist and reporter while taking night courses at Columbia and the School of Visual Arts. He got his start drawing small sports illustrations, but in 1960, after the death of his mentor Leo O'Melia, he became the paper's primary sports cartoonist. In his 50 years as a cartoonist for the *Daily News*, he contributed over 15,000 cartoons.

In 1998, he received the Milton Caniff Lifetime Achievement Award, was inducted into the International Boxing Hall of Fame and the Baseball Hall of Fame put his work in their permanent collection. On May 7, 2011, he received the Ellis Island Medal of Honor. He passed away a few days later on May 10, 2011, at the age of 88.

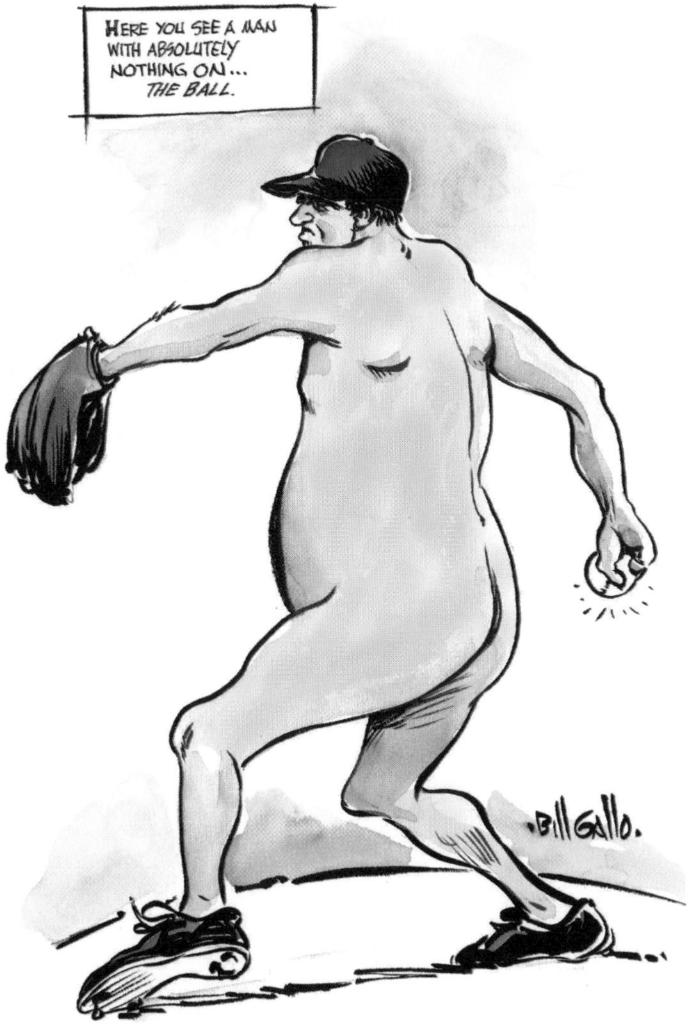
HERE YOU SEE A MAN WITH ABSOLUTELY NOTHING ON... THE BALL.
Bill Gallo.

Rick Geary (b. 1946, Kansas City, MO) attended the University of Kansas, where he received a bachelor's degree in communications and a master's degree in film. After college, Geary became a freelance artist. In 1977 Geary got his cartooning start in the *National Lampoon* "Funny Pages," and was a regular contributor for 13 years. His illustrations were also published in many periodicals including *Mad*, *New York Times Book Review*, *Spy*, *The Los Angeles Times* and *Rolling Stone*. Geary has also written and illustrated numerous children's books and comics, including the long-running comic series *A Treasury Of Victorian Murder*. Geary lives with his wife in Carrizozo, NM.

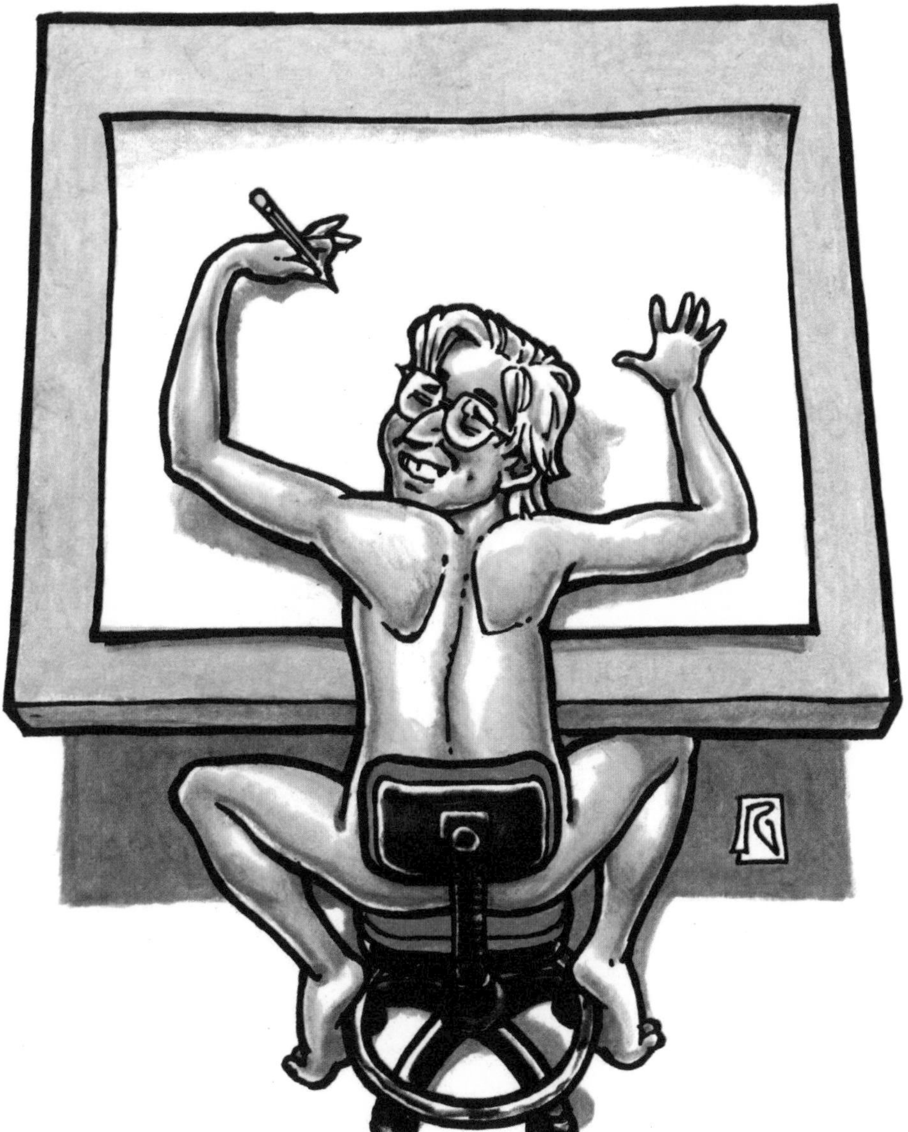

Stan Goldberg (b. 1932, NY) began his comics career at age 16 in 1949, working as a colorist and eventual color designer for Marvel Comics, where he created the signature color schemes of all Marvel superheroes and villains of the 1960s, including Spider-Man, the Fantastic Four, The X-Men and The Hulk. Goldberg's work has appeared in *National Lampoon, Child, Redbook, Seventeen, Ms.* and *Working Woman*, but he is best known for his work for Archie Comics. Recently, he has illustrated *The Simpsons* for Bongo Comics, and has a collection, *The Best of Stan Goldburg* from Archie Comics.

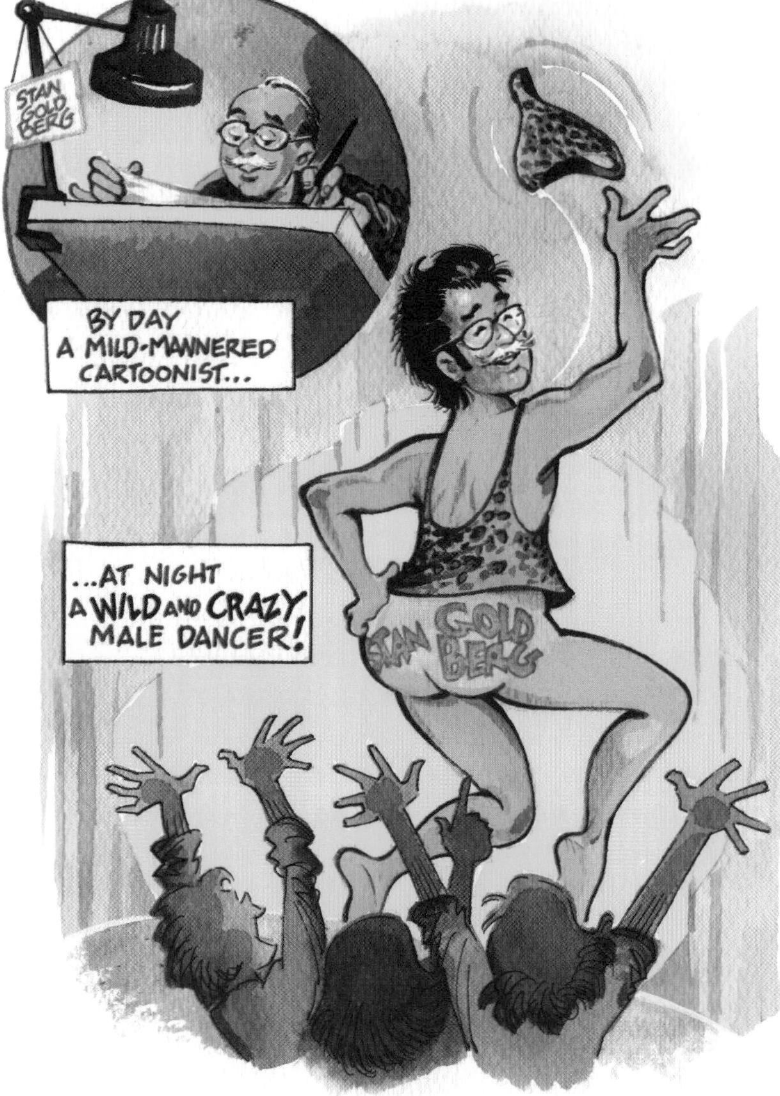
STAN GOLD BERG
BY DAY A MILD-MANNERED CARTOONIST...
...AT NIGHT A WILD AND CRAZY MALE DANCER!
STAN GOLD BERG

Bud Grace (b. 1944, Chester, PA) grew up in Florida and attended Florida State University, where he received a Ph. D in physics in 1971. After working at FSU as a nuclear physicist, Grace realized he was in the wrong line of work, so in 1979 he became a cartoonist. Grace freelanced for several magazines, and in 1988, he created his own newspaper comic strip, *Ernie* (which became a very popular bi-monthly comic in Sweden and Norway). *Ernie* was later changed to *The Pirahna Club* in the U.S. in 1998. Grace is also known for working on another King Feature comic strip, *Babs & Aldo*, under the pseudonym Buddy Valentine. The Swedish Academy of Comic Art awarded the Adamson Statuette to Grace in 1989. In 1993 Grace also was awarded the National Cartoonists Society Newspaper Comic Strip Award for *Ernie*.

DISCUS
BOYISH GRIN
BUTTOCKS
FOR MARK.
THIS IS HOW I
LOOK NAKED.
AT LEAST THE
LAST TIME I
HAD THE NERVE
TO CHECK — BUD

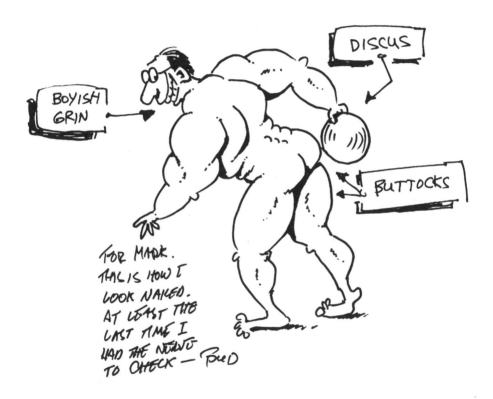

Samuel H. Gross (b. 1933, NY) is the son of two Eastern European immigrants. He has been cartooning for over six decades for clients such as *The New Yorker*, *Harvard Business Review*, *Esquire*, *Cosmopolitan* and *Good Housekeeping*. Gross has worked as Cartoon Editor for the *National Lampoon* and taught multiple semesters at the Pratt Institute. His work is collected in *I am Blind and My Dog is Dead*, *We Have Ways of Making You Laugh: 120 Swastika Cartoons* and *The Complete Cartoons of the New Yorker*. Gross lives in New York City with his wife Isabelle.

S.GROSS

Etta Hulme (b. 1923, Somerville, TX) attended the University of Texas, earning a degree in Fine Arts. After a stint in animation at the Walt Disney Studios, Hulme moved to Chicago, where she drew the *Red Rabbit* comic books. Hulme returned to Texas in the 1950s, where she met her husband Vernon Hulme. She freelanced for the *Texas Observer* before she became a full-time editorial cartoonist for *The Fort Worth Star-Telegram* in 1972. Her political cartoons, which have since become nationally syndicated, earned her The National Cartoonists Society award for Best Editorial Cartoonist in 1982, the first time the award was given to a woman. She won the award again in 1998, and was the 1987 President of the Association of American Editorial Cartoonists.

ETTA HULME

Al Jaffee (b. 1921, Savannah, GA) got his first job in the comics industry in 1941 at Quality Comics, where he was the artist and writer for *Inferior Man*. He worked on funny animal comics as a cartoonist and editor at Timely before moving to *Mad* magazine in 1955. He invented the *Mad* Fold-In in 1964 and is now the magazine's oldest regular contributor. Jaffee has received several awards from the National Cartoonists Society: the Special Features Award in 1971 and 1975; the Advertising and Illustration Award in 1973; and the Humor Comic Book Award in 1979. He also won the Cartoonist of the Year Reuben award in 2008. Jaffee and his wife, Joyce, reside in New York City.

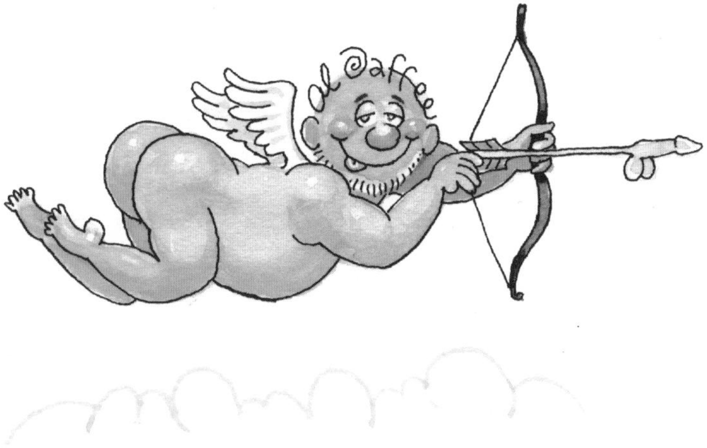
Al Jaffee

For Mark Cohen & Rosie McDaniel with Love – Al J.

Michael Jantze (b. 1962 in Middletown, NY) spent his childhood in Normal, IL. After a stint as an art director, he created the syndicated comic strip *The Norm*. An alumnus of Goshen College and California State University Northridge, he currently teaches at the Savannah College of Art and Design.

Lynn Johnston (b. 1947, Collingwood, Ontario, Canada) grew up in North Vancouver, B.C. She attended the Vancouver School of Art. She was a medial artist for McMaster University in Hamilton, Ontario before she began drawing single-panel cartoons, which were later collected into three books. Johnston and her second husband, Rod Johnston, moved to Lynn Lake, Manitoba, where she created the popular comic strip *For Better or For Worse* for Universal Press in 1979, which is currently read in more than 2000 newspapers worldwide. Johnston has won numerous awards including the Reuben Award from the National Cartoonists Society in 1985, the Order of Canada in 1993 and the Canadian Cartoonist Hall of Fame in 2008. She was nominated for a Pulitzer Prize in 1993 for her story about her character Lawrence's coming out.

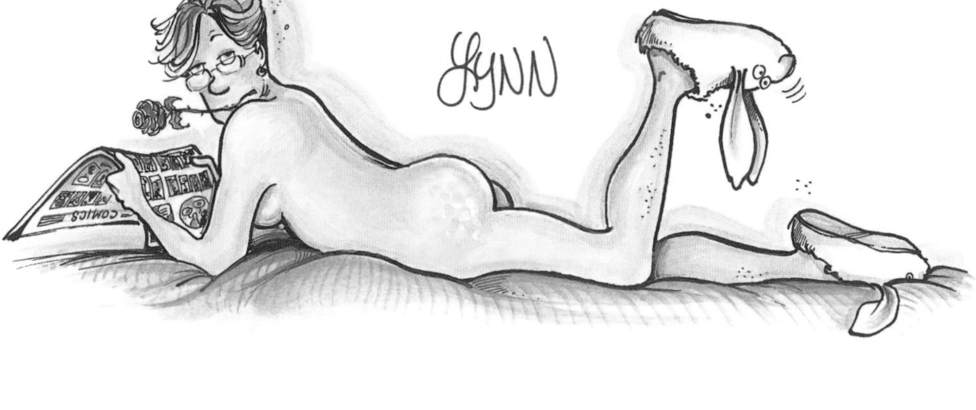
LYNN

Buck Jones (b. 1961), inspired by *Mad* magazine, began illustrating his high school and Truman State University newspapers, winning various local awards and earning a reputation for humor and gag comics. In 1985 he became a full-time illustrator working on advertisements, gag comics, books, educational materials, magazines and greeting cards. His list of clients over the years has included *Cat Fancy*, Chrysler Corporation, Gatorade, Kodak, Better Homes & Gardens Books, Scholastic Publishing, Carnival Cruises and many more. The National Cartoonists Society nominated Jones for an award in its book division in 2003. He currently lives in Des Moines, IA with his wife and two children.

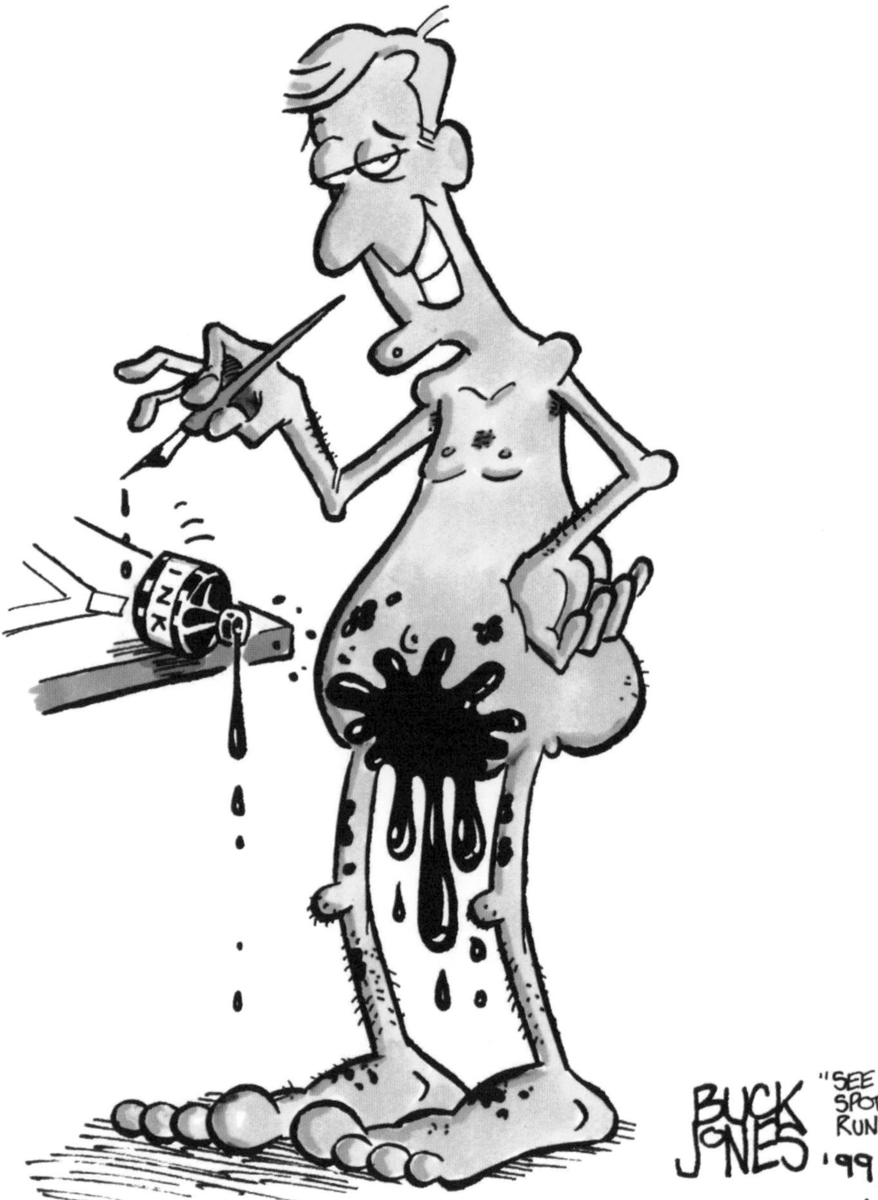
INK
BUCK JONES "SEE SPOT RUN" '99
TO MARKY!

Bil Keane (1922-2011, Philadelphia, PA) taught himself to draw during his high school years. He served in the Army from 1942 to 1945, during which time he drew for *Yank* and *Stars and Stripes*. He married Thelma Carne in 1948, and the couple had five children. From 1946 to 1959 Keane worked as a staff artist for *The Philadelphia Bulletin*, where he created his first regular comic strip, *Silly Philly*.

Keane's first syndicated strip, *Channel Chuckles*, made its debut in 1954 and ran for 23 years. *Family Circus*, the daily newspaper panel for which Keane is best known, began in 1960. Keane won the National Cartoonists Society's Award for Best Syndicated Panel four times during the '60s and '70s and received the society's Reuben Award in 1982. Keane died in 2011 at his home in Arizona.

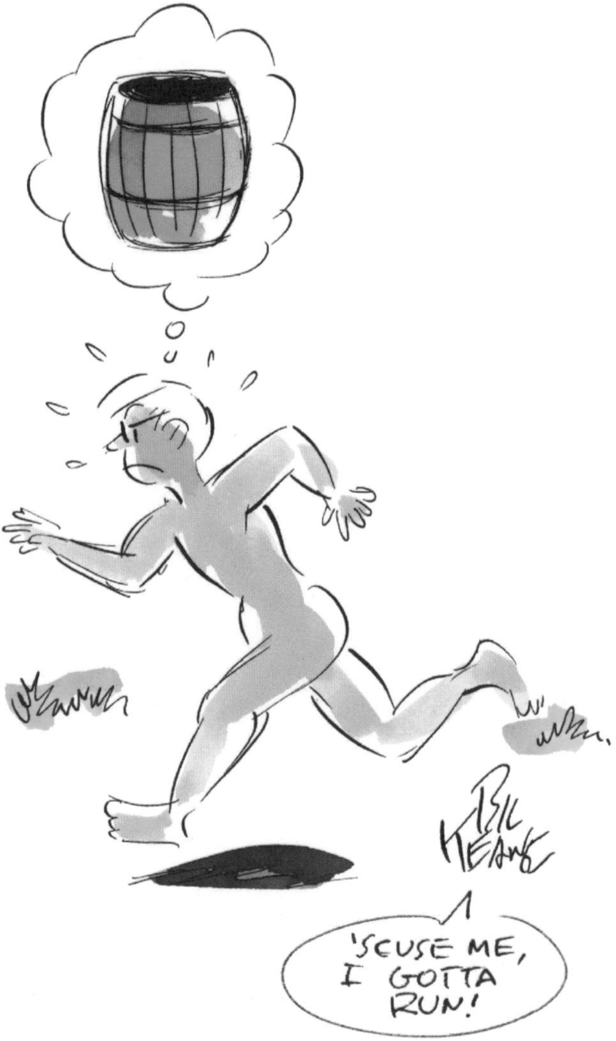
'SCUSE ME, I GOTTA RUN!

Jeff Keane (b. 1958, Philadelphia, PA) is the youngest son of *The Family Circus* creator Bil Keane. He was a model for his father's illustrations prior to the series' launch on Feb. 29, 1960. The comic strip made its debut in 19 newspapers and is now featured in over 1,500. Jeff Keane attended the University of Southern California, where he received a B.F.A. in Drama. In 1981, he returned to assist his father in the production of *The Family Circus* by penciling, inking, coloring, writing gags and much more. Keane currently resides in Laguna Hills, CA with his wife and three children, and continues to draw *The Family Circus*.

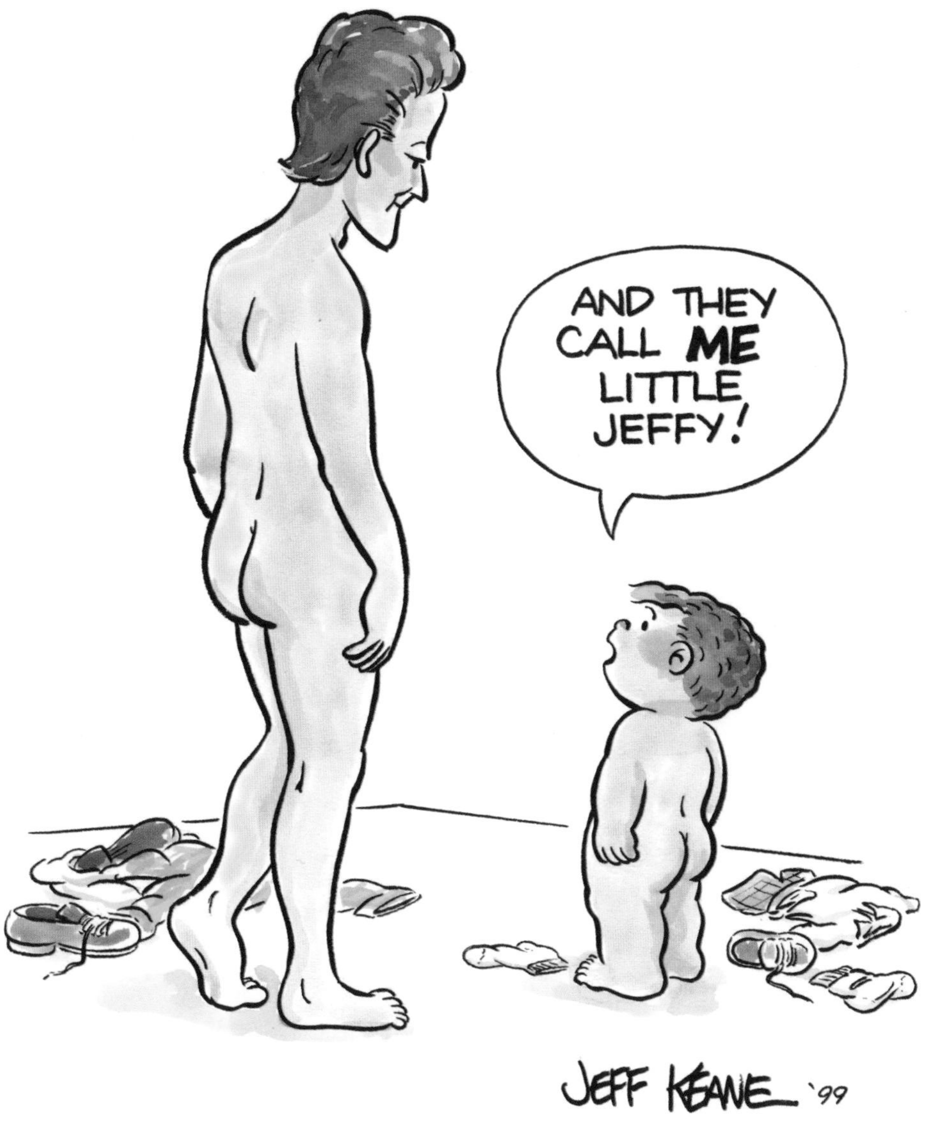
AND THEY CALL ME LITTLE JEFFY!
JEFF KEANE '99

Polly Keener (b. 1946, Akron, OH) studied at Kent State University, Connecticut College and Princeton University. She began freelance cartooning in 1977, and created strips that mostly featured animal characters parodying daily human life. *Hamster Alley* was the most successful of these. Keener's other popular strip is the puzzle comic *Mystery Mosaic*. Between them, *Hamster Alley* and *Mystery Mosaic* have run in over 450 newspapers. In 1992, Keener wrote a cartoon how-to book called *Cartooning*. She also wrote *The Writer's Little Instruction Book: 385 Secrets for Writing Well and Getting Published*. Keener has won awards and taught cartooning at the University of Akron.

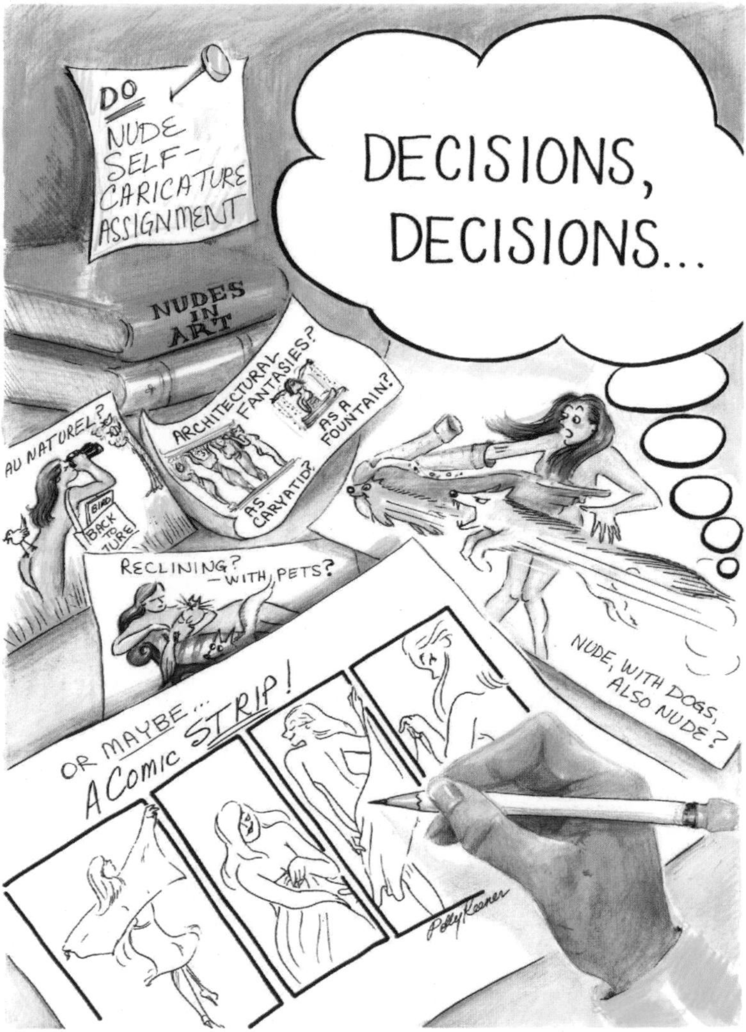
DO
NUDE SELF-CARICATURE ASSIGNMENT
DECISIONS, DECISIONS...
NUDES IN ART
ARCHITECTURAL FANTASIES?
AS A FOUNTAIN?
AS CARYATID?
AU NATUREL?
BIRD
RECLINING? —WITH PETS?
NUDE, WITH DOGS, ALSO NUDE?
OR MAYBE... A COMIC STRIP!
Polly Keener

For Rosie + Mark, with best wishes! Polly (Keener) 1999

Richard Kirkman (b. 1953, NC) learned to draw by imitating *Peanuts, Pogo* and *Dennis the Menace*. In junior high he produced a parody of *Mad*. After some encouraging words from a high school teacher, Kirkman attended college and graduated with a two-year degree in Advertising Art. He worked as a graphic designer and illustrator for a couple years before meeting Jerry Scott. Their friendship and parenting experiences eventually led them to their collaborative series, *Baby Blues*. Creators Syndicate first published the series in 1990, and later King Features Syndicate helped it spread to over 1,200 newspapers worldwide. Kirkman and his wife currently live in Arizona.

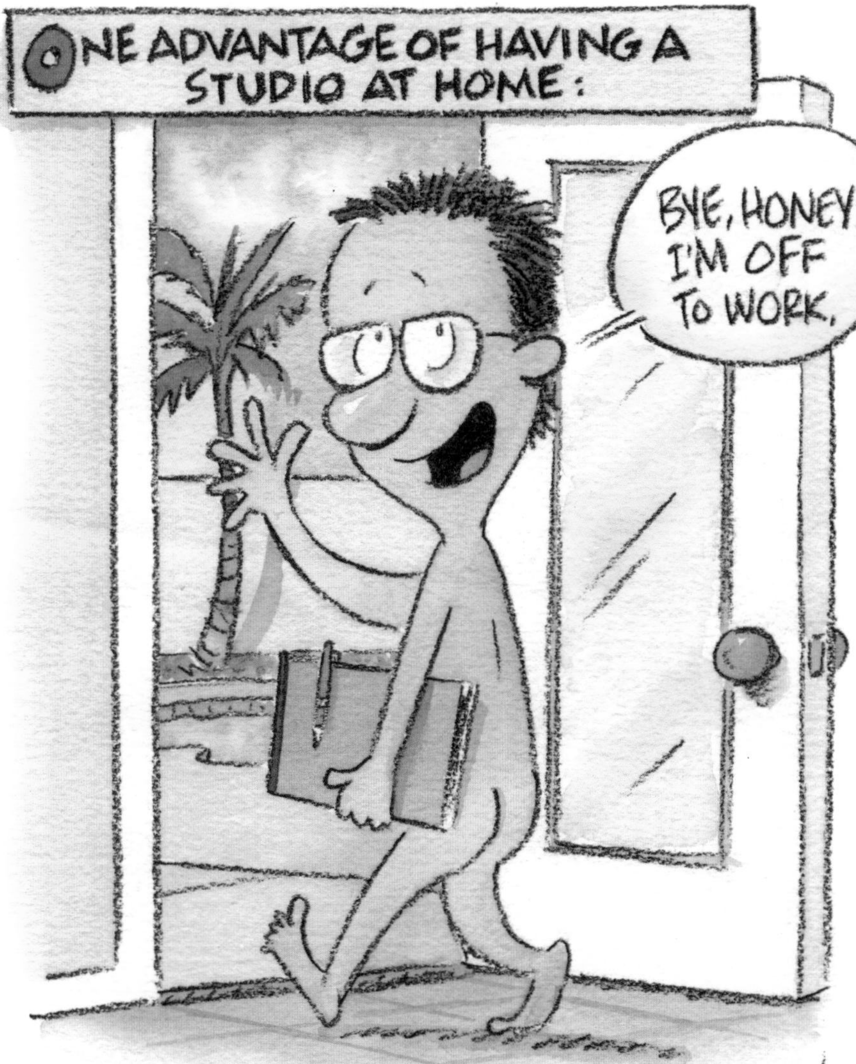
ONE ADVANTAGE OF HAVING A STUDIO AT HOME:
BYE, HONEY! I'M OFF TO WORK.
RICK KIRKMAN

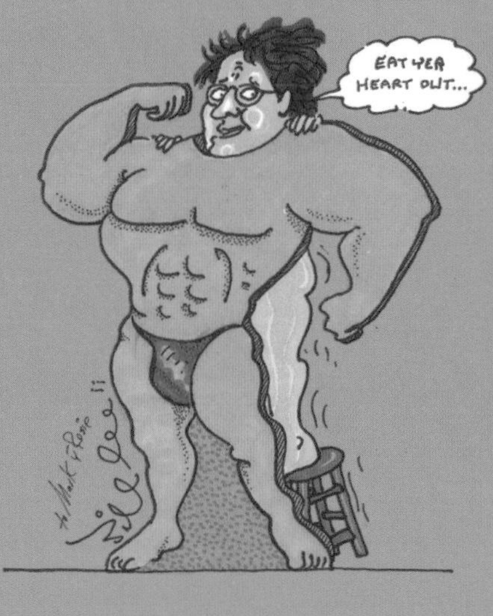
EAT YER
HEART OUT...

Bill Lee's cartoons have appeared in *The New York Times* op-ed page, and he has been the humor editor of publications and websites such as *Penthouse*, *Omni* and *Forum*. Lee has written a screenplay for CBS, and his cartoon art has been collected in seven books. He has traveled around the world on assignment for his "Investigative Cartooning" features, and has received four awards for his work. Lee has a wife, Dona, and a daughter, Jennifer Catherine.

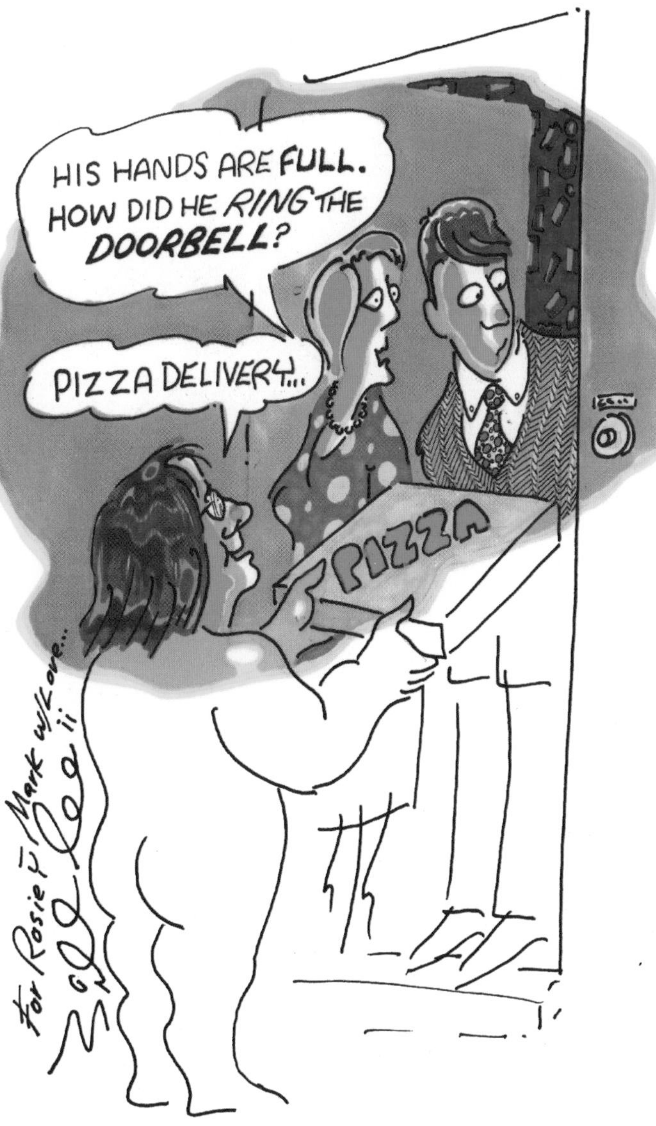
HIS HANDS ARE FULL. HOW DID HE RING THE DOORBELL?
PIZZA DELIVERY...
PIZZA
For Rosie & Mark w/Love...

Arnold "Arnie" Levin (b. 1938, Brooklyn, NY) moved to Miami in 1950, where he studied commercial art at Miami Technical High School. He entered the U.S. Marine Corps after graduation. In 1958 he returned to New York and studied at the Art Students League before becoming the animation director for Electra Studio. He began doing cartoons and cover art for *The New Yorker* in 1974. Levin won the Gag Cartoon Award from the National Cartoonists Society in 1991 and 1992. He has taught at the School of Visual Arts, Pratt Institute and Long Island University. He currently works in computer animation and video.

To Mark and Rosie... Best *[signature]*

Lee Lorenz (b. 1932, Hackensack, NJ) is a gag cartoonist and professional jazz cornet player. He studied at Carnegie Tech and Pratt Institute. After freelancing gag cartoons for a variety of magazines, including *Collier's*, in the 1950s, he began his long association with *The New Yorker*, not only as a cartoonist, but eventually as an art director and chronicler of the magazine and its contributors. Lorenz resides in Easton, CT.

L'APRES MIDI D'UNE CARTOONISTE

Gary McCoy had a deep love for cartoons at an early age. McCoy worked for the *Suburban Journals Of Greater St. Louis* as an editorial cartoonist. The work McCoy did in the *Journals* would later be reprinted by other publications, including school textbooks, *The Washington Post* and *The Best Editorial Cartoons Of The Year*. McCoy is the primary cartoonist for the Romanian magazine *Vivid* and works as a freelance cartoonist, graphic artist and humor illustrator for numerous companies, including *ABC. com*, *Gibson Greetings* and *Playboy*. McCoy has received numerous nominations from the National Cartoonists Society, including "Best Gag Cartoonist" and "Best Greeting Card Cartoonist." After a long career as a freelance artist, McCoy created the syndicated comic panel *The Flying McCoys* with his brother, Glen. McCoy is also a stand-up comedian, and won HBO's *Stand-Up Stand-Off* competition. McCoy currently resides in Belleville, IL.

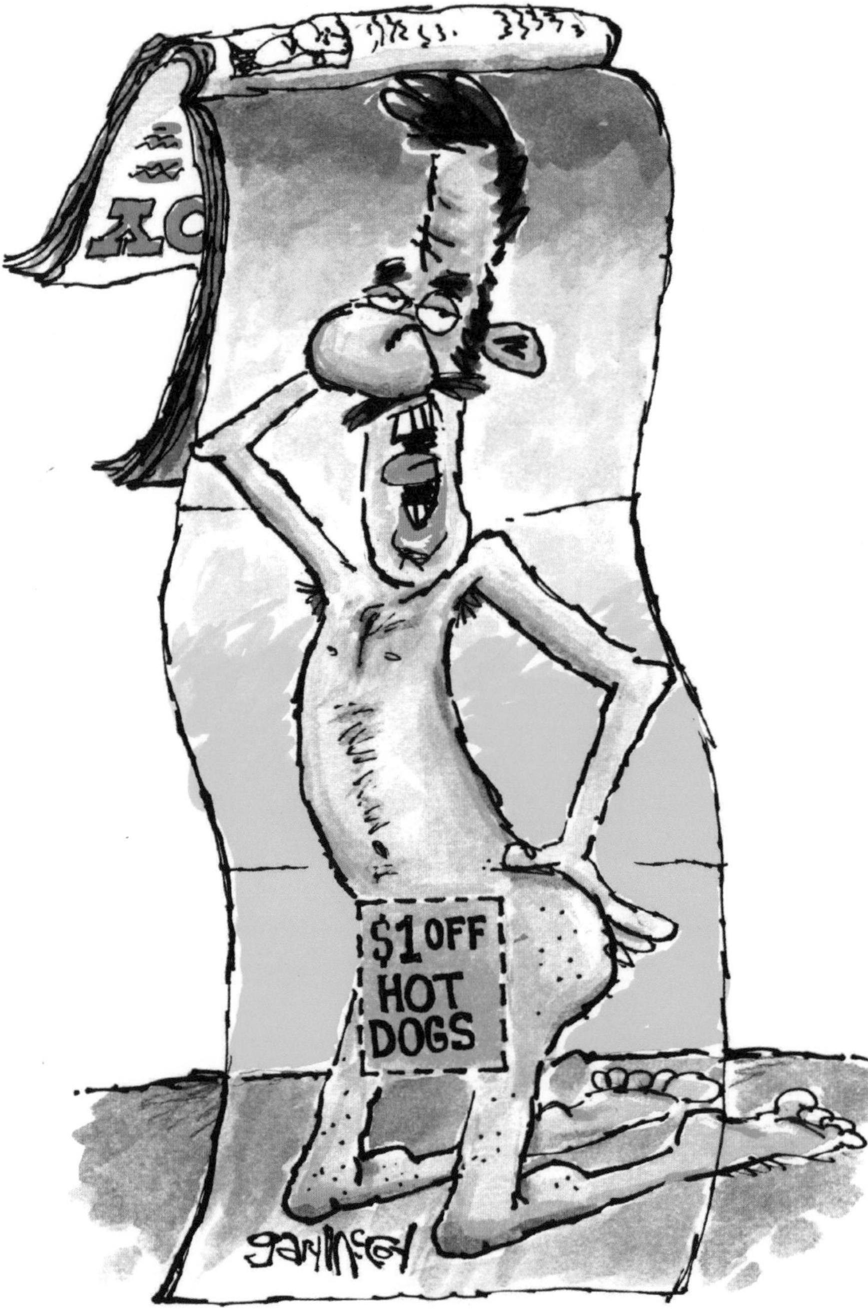
$1 OFF
HOT
DOGS
garyMcCoy

David Wiley Miller (b. 1951, Burbank, CA) is the cartoonist behind the popular newspaper strip *Non Sequitur*, which he signs as "Wiley." He worked as an editorial cartoonist at the *Greensboro News & Record* and the *San Francisco Examiner* before beginning *Non Sequitur* in 1991. Miller has won several awards for his editorial cartooning, including the Robert F. Kennedy Journalism Award in 1991. For *Non Sequitur*, Miller became the first cartoonist to win the National Cartoonists Society's Newspaper Comic Strip Award in his first year of syndication. Miller, his wife Victoria Coviello and their four Jack Russell terriers, live in Kennebunkport, ME.

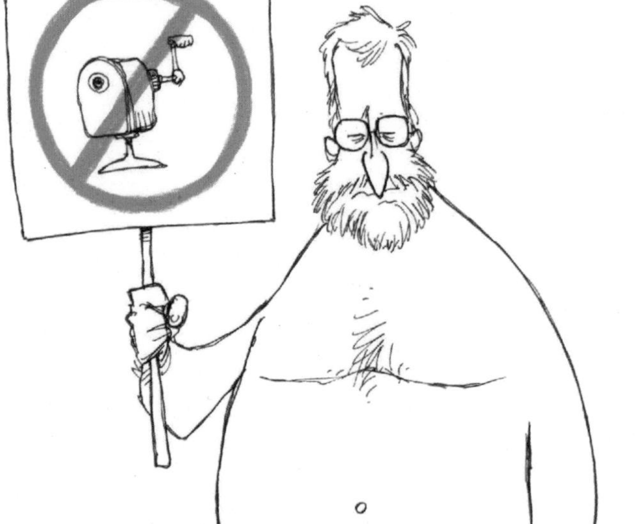
WILEY
EXPOSED

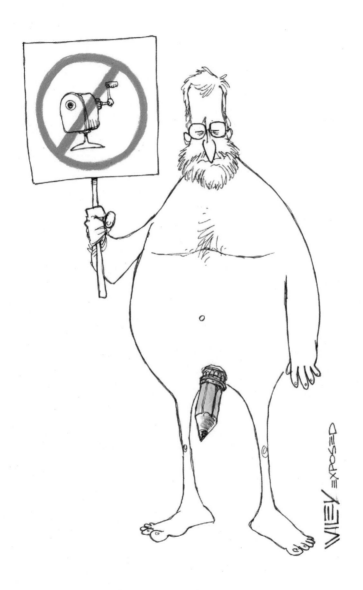

Russell Myers (b. 1938, Pittsburgh, KS) is best known for his newspaper strip *Broom-Hilda*, which launched in the *Chicago Tribune* in April of 1970. He grew up in the college town of Tulsa, OK. and worked as an illustrator for Hallmark Cards before *Broom-Hilda*'s debut. The award-winning strip chronicles the adventures of a warty, 1,500-year-old-witch. Myers, a car collector, lives with his wife in Oregon.

History is strangely silent regarding the handsome and charismatic cartoonist, Lord Godiva. (a.k.a. RUSSELL MYERS)

Tim "Mr. Ollie" Oliphant (b. 1961, Nashville, TN) spent his youth teaching himself how to draw by copying the Sunday comics and *Mad* magazine. After high school, he attended a small art school in Franklin, TN to pursue a career as a letterer, but instead chose to pursue freelance cartooning. He began creating a diverse body of editorial cartoons, humorous illustrations, caricatures and greeting cards. Since 1987, he has been a teaching artist and an artist-in-residence through the Tennessee Arts Commission and has taught in schools across the country. Oliphant is a member of the National Cartoonists Society and served as an Educational Committee Chairman for 10 years. He was awarded the School Bell Award by the Tennessee Education Association for his education-related editorial cartoons. His illustrations have appeared in *The Saturday Evening Post*, *Woman's World*, *Boy's Life* and *Highlights for Kids*. Mr. Ollie resides in the countryside of Lewisburg, TN.

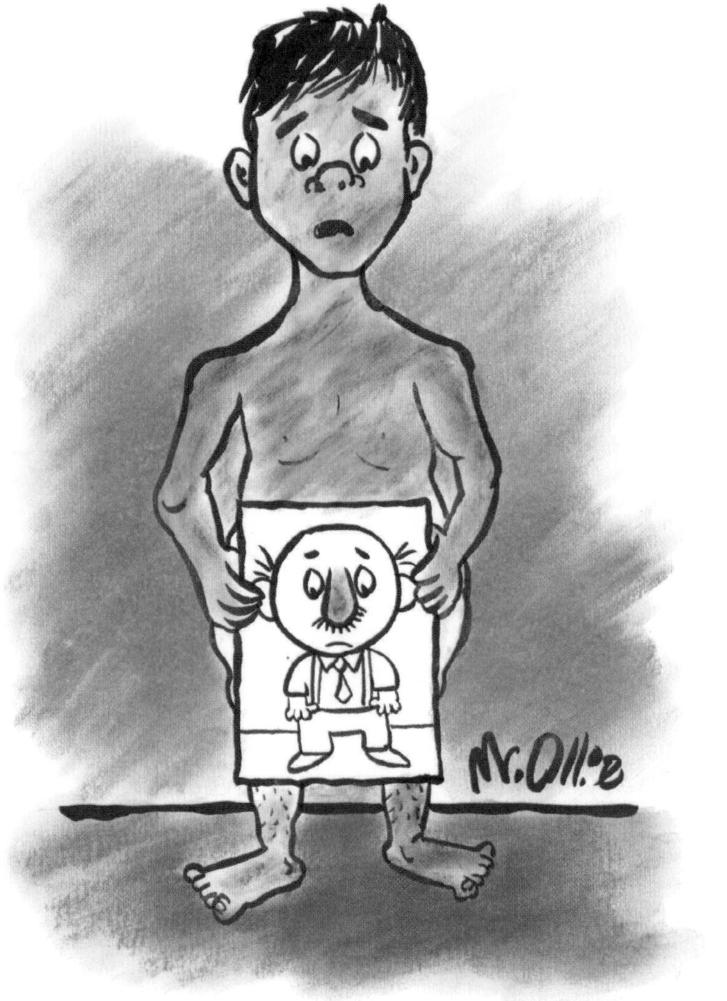
Mr. Oll.'02

Nina Paley (b. 1968, Urbana, IL) began her career in 1988 with her semi-autobiographical comic strip *Nina's Adventure*. The strip ran for seven years, was featured in magazines such as *Santa Cruz Comic News*, *LA Reader* and the *San Francisco Examiner* and has been compiled in two books. After the end of *Nina's Adventures*, Paley created a new strip, *Fluff*. Paley's other comic pieces have been featured in various anthologies by Last Gasp, Rip Off Press and Dark Horse Comics. Besides comics, Paley is an award-winning one-woman animator whose projects include *Fetch!*, *The Stork* and *Sita Sings The Blues*. She has taught animation at the Parsons School of Design and earned a 2006 Guggenheim Fellowship.

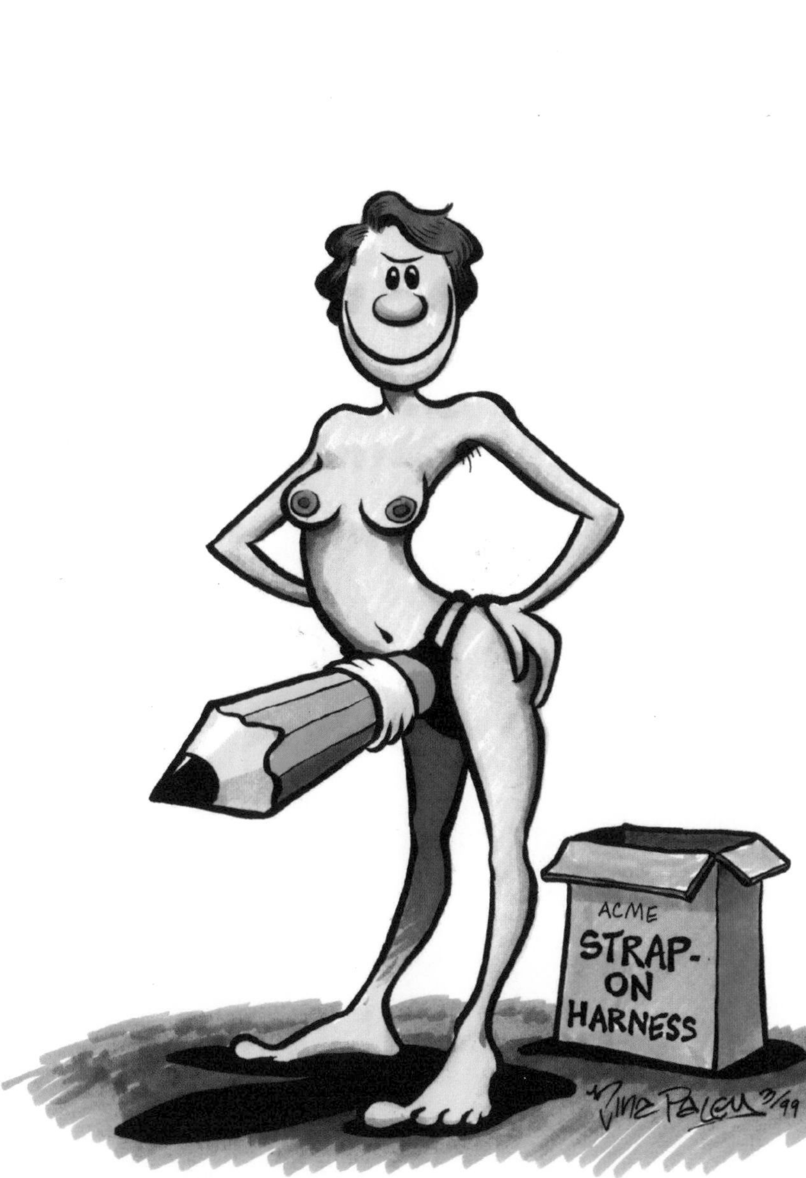
ACME
STRAP-
ON
HARNESS

Roy E. Peterson (b. 1936, Winnipeg, Canada) is best known for his editorial cartoons for *The Vancouver Sun* (1962-2009). His work also appears in *Maclean's* magazine, illustrating a column by Allan Fotheringham. Peterson has also illustrated the covers for many of Fotheringham's books. He authored *The World According to Roy Peterson*, *Drawn and Quartered*, and *Peterson's ABCs*. Peterson has won seven National Newspaper Awards and became an Officer of the Order of Canada in 2004.

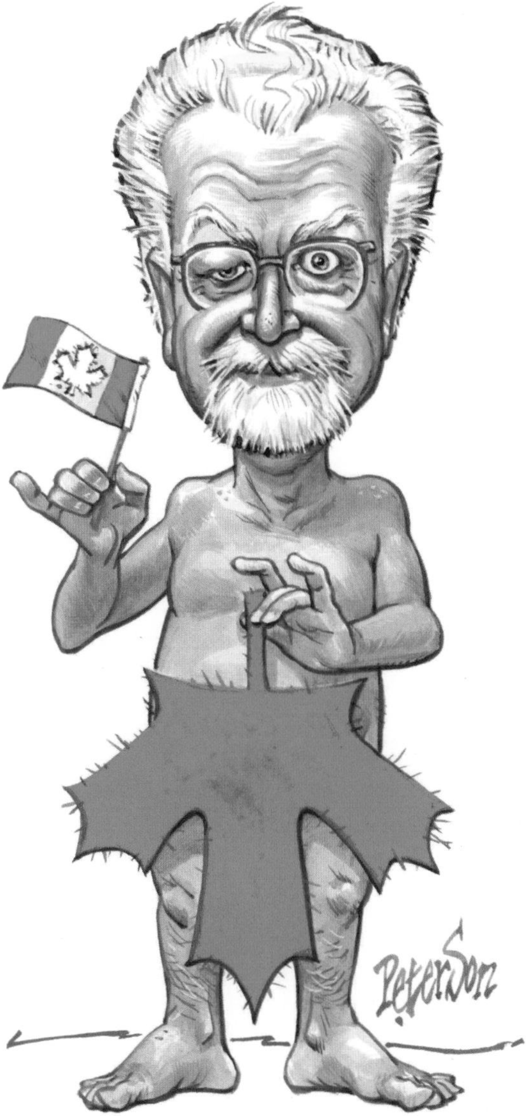
Peterson

ROY'S NAKED PATRIOTISM
WAS EXCEEDED ONLY BY HIS
FERTILE IMAGINATION.

Dan Piraro (b. 1958, Kansas City, MO) was raised in Tulsa, OK. In 1976, Piraro attended and graduated from Booker T. Washington High School. Piraro then attended, but later dropped out of, Washington University in St. Louis. While living in Dallas, TX in 1985 Piraro began to work on his cartoon panel *Bizarro* which he sold to syndication. It appears in more than 250 papers and has been reprinted in 15 books. Piraro is a very political vegan who conveys a lot of his views through the *Bizarro* strip. He has also created T-shirt designs to raise money for a non-profit organization called The Woodland Farm Animal Sanctuary, which is committed to stopping abuse of animals used for food. In 2001, Piraro began touring with his one-man comedy show entitled *The Bizarro Baloney Show*, which received the 2002 New York International Fringe Festival's award for Best Solo Show. Piraro was also awarded The National Cartoonists Society's Panel Cartoon Award in 1999, 2000 and 2001 and a Reuben Award in 2010.

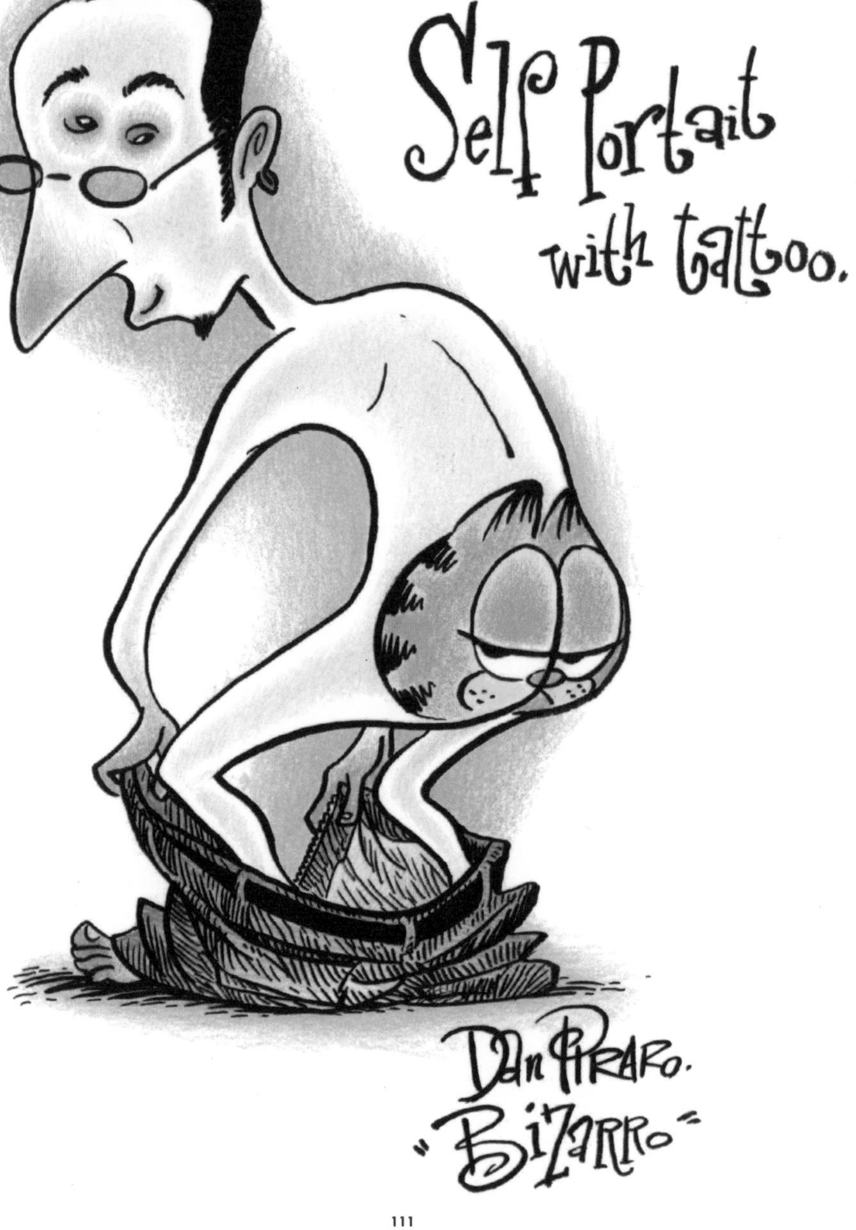
Self Portait
with tattoo.
Dan Piraro.
"Bizarro"

Peter Paul Porges (b. 1927, Vienna, Austria) was passionate about American cartooning as a child. During Hitler's rule, Porges spent time in an internment camp before escaping to Switzerland, where he studied art. He made his way to America, only to be drafted by the U.S. Army and sent back overseas. After the war was over, his family emigrated to the U.S., where they lived in New York City. In 1954, Porges drew for the *Saturday Evening Post*, then for *Mad* magazine, the *Saturday Review of Literature* and *The New Yorker*. He and his wife, Lucie, currently live in New York's Upper West Side.

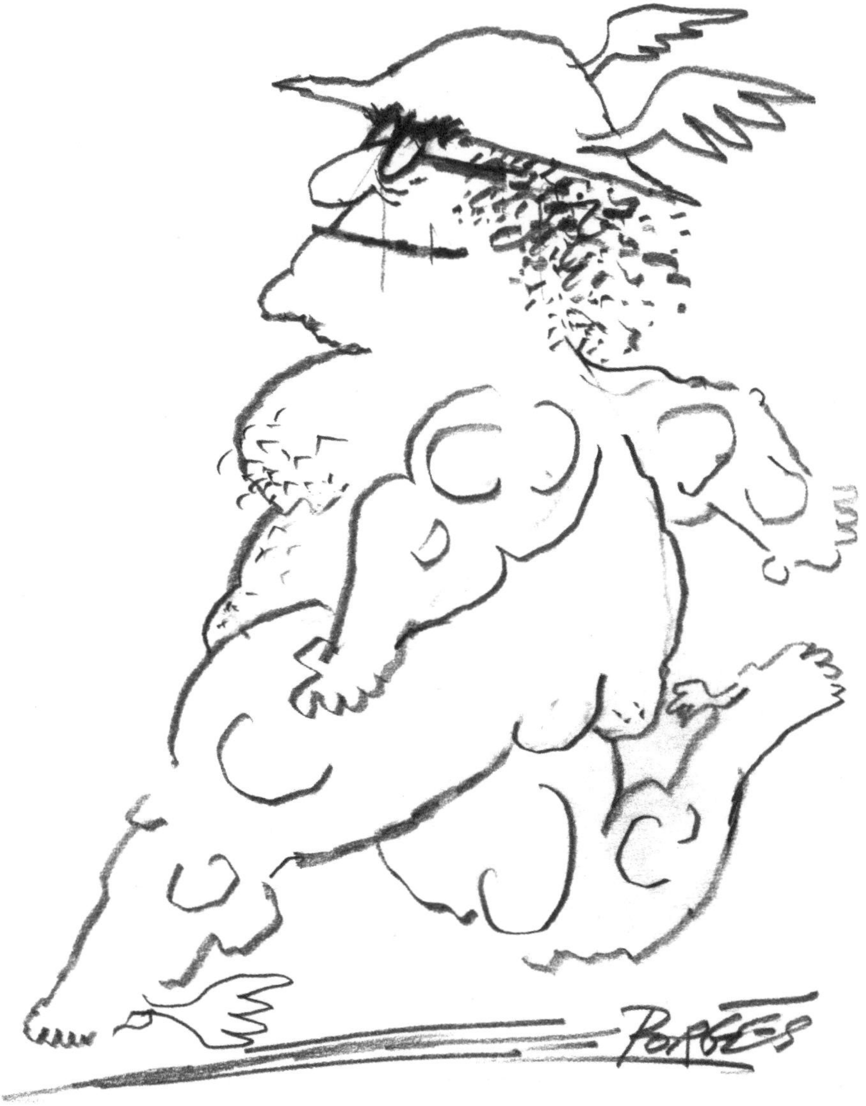
BORGES

Trina Robbins (b. 1938) is best known for *It Ain't Me, Babe* and *Wimmen's Comix*. She was one of the earliest female cartoonists in the underground comix movement in the 1970s. She was instrumental in promoting and fostering women cartoonists and helped create the aforementioned *Wimmen's Comix*, the influential all-women cartoonists anthology that addressed feminist concerns and political issues. In the 1980s, Robbins did a stint as a penciler on *Wonder Woman* for DC. Robbins is also the author and editor of several histories of women cartoonists, including *A Century of Women Cartoonists* and *From Girls to Grrrlz: A History of Women's Comics from Teens to Zines*. She lives in San Francisco.

Arnold Roth (b. 1929, Philadelphia, PA) graduated from the University of the Arts in 1950 and began freelancing in 1951. His cartoons and illustrations appeared in *Trump*, *Humbug* — which he co-published - and *Help!* He was also a regular contributor to *Playboy* and *National Lampoon*. His work has been featured on the cover of *The New Yorker*, as well as in *Time*, *Sports Illustrated* and *Esquire*. He also drew the Sunday strip *Poor Arnold's Almanac* from 1959 to 1961.

Roth received numerous awards from the National Cartoonists Society throughout the '70s and '80s, as well as their Gold Key Award in 2000. He was inducted in the Society of Illustrators Hall of Fame in 2009. His art is in the collections of museums such as the Museum of Cartoon Art in San Francisco, the Philadelphia Museum of Art and the Caricature and Cartoon Museum in Basel, Switzerland. He and his wife, Caroline, live in New York City and have two sons.

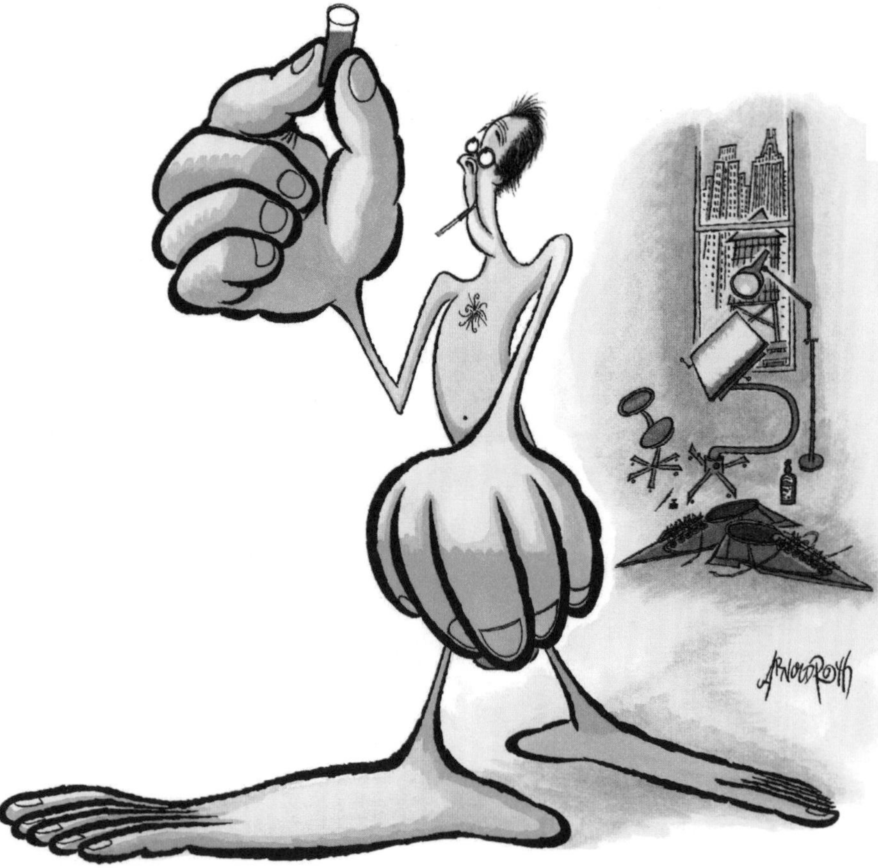
ARNOLD ROTH

Howie Schneider (1930-2007, USA) was a Massachusetts-based cartoonist, sculptor and children's book author best known for his comic strip *Eek & Meek*, which ran for 35 years in over 400 newspapers across the country. Schneider's other strips included *Percy's World* and *Bimbo's Circus*, also known as *The Circus of P.T. Bimbo*. After *Eek & Meek* was canceled, Schneider joined the *Provincetown Banner* as its editorial cartoonist. During this time he also published the cartoon books *Howie Schneider Unshucked*, *The World is no Place for Children* and *Mom's the Word*. In 2003, he launched a daily comic strip called *The Sunshine Club*, which ran until his death in 2007.

Schneider's cartoons were also featured in numerous magazines, such as *The New Yorker*, *Playboy*, *Esquire*, *Redbook* and *McCall's*. His work for these publications made him a two-time winner of Best Editorial Cartoon from the New England Press Association. He also served on the board of the Newspaper Features Council for 20 years and on the board of the National Cartoonists Society for eight years.

Just another Burgher!

Charles Monroe Schulz (1922–2000, Minneapolis, MN)'s first published comic was a sketch of his dog Spike (later to be the inspiration for Snoopy). After serving in the Army, Schulz returned to St. Paul, where The Pioneer Press ran his one-panel comic *Lil' Folks* from 1947–1950. United Features Syndicate bought *Lil' Folks* in 1950 and renamed the strip *Peanuts*. Schulz settled in California in 1958 with his first wife, Joyce, and five children.

Schulz won two Reuben Awards, received a star on the Hollywood Walk of Fame, was inducted into the Museum of Cartoon Art Hall of Fame, and has been granted the Milton Caniff Lifetime Achievement Award and a Congressional Gold Medal, awarded posthumously in June, 2001. More than 2,600 newspapers worldwide carried *Peanuts*, when he announced his retirement in December, 1999. In 2002 his widow, Jean, presided at the opening of the Charles M. Schulz Muzeum and Research Center in Santa Rosa, CA where they lived for the last twenty-six years of his life.

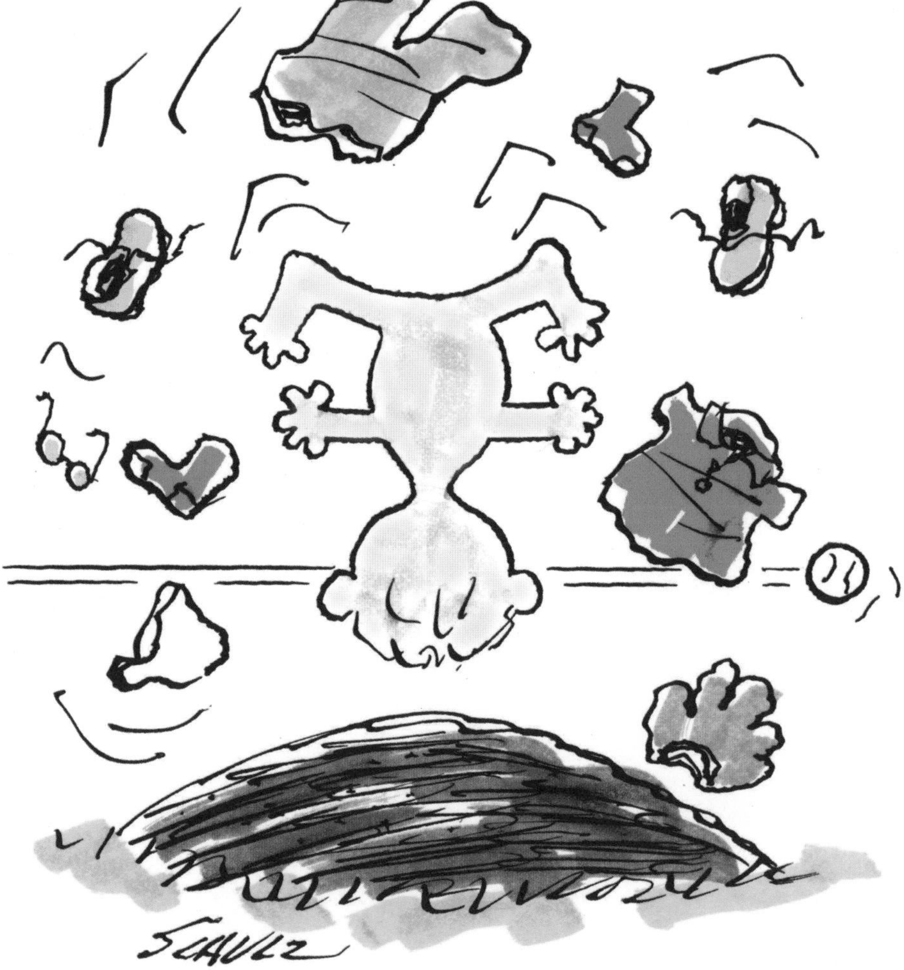
SCHULZ

Harley L. Schwadron graduated from Bowdoin College in Maine and from UC Berkeley with a master's in journalism. He began as a reporter for the *Hartford Times* in Connecticut, and then a public relations news writer and college alumni magazine editor at the University of Michigan. While working at the university, he began doing freelance cartoons for international magazines. He specializes in business cartoons and *9 to 5* is his syndicated one-panel cartoon. He was also a regular contributor to *Punch* and has done op-ed work in *The Washington Post, The Washington Times, The Dayton Daily News, The Los Angeles Times* and *The Des Moines Register*. He currently resides in Ann Arbor, MI.

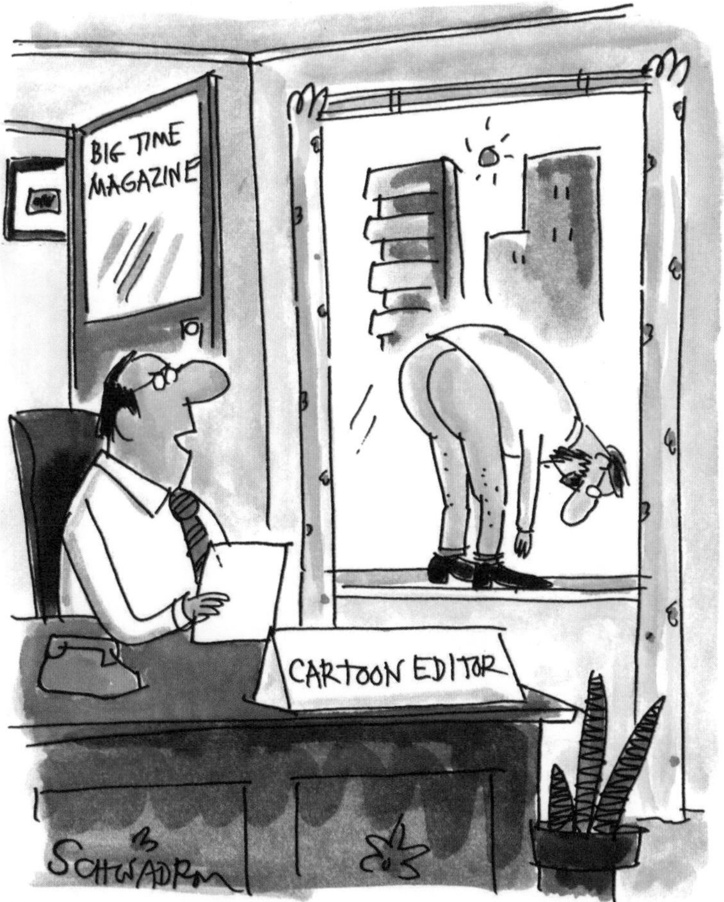
BIG TIME MAGAZINE
CARTOON EDITOR
SCHWADRON
"DAMMIT, SCHWADRON! I THOUGHT I'D NEVER SEE YOU AGAIN WHEN I STOPPED USING YOUR CARTOONS!"

Howard Shoemaker (b. 1931, Council Bluffs, IA) works in animation, design, advertising and cartooning. He is not formally trained in art. He contributed cartoons to the controversial *The Realist*, as well as publications such as *Road and Track* and *Jazz*. He is best known for his *Playboy* comics, collected in *Goodbye, Cruel World* (1972). Shoemaker also created a Porsche-enthusiast-themed cartoon book. He settled in Omaha, NE, with his wife and four children.

Jeff Smith (b. 1960, Columbus, OH) grew up in McKees Rocks, PA. Smith began self-publishing the comic book *Bone* in 1991, which became one of the flagship creator-owned, black-and-white, independent comics of the 1990s. *Bone*, and Smith, have won numerous Eisner and Harvey Awards and two National Cartoonists Society awards. In 2008, he began self-publishing another series, *RASL*. He has also authored *Shazam! The Monster Society for Evil* for DC Comics, created the children's book *Little Mouse Gets Ready* and drawn the covers to *Walt Kelly's Our Gang* for Fantagraphics. There have been exhibitions of his work, and in 2009 he was the subject of the documentary *The Cartoonist: Jeff Smith, Bone and the Changing Face of Comics.*

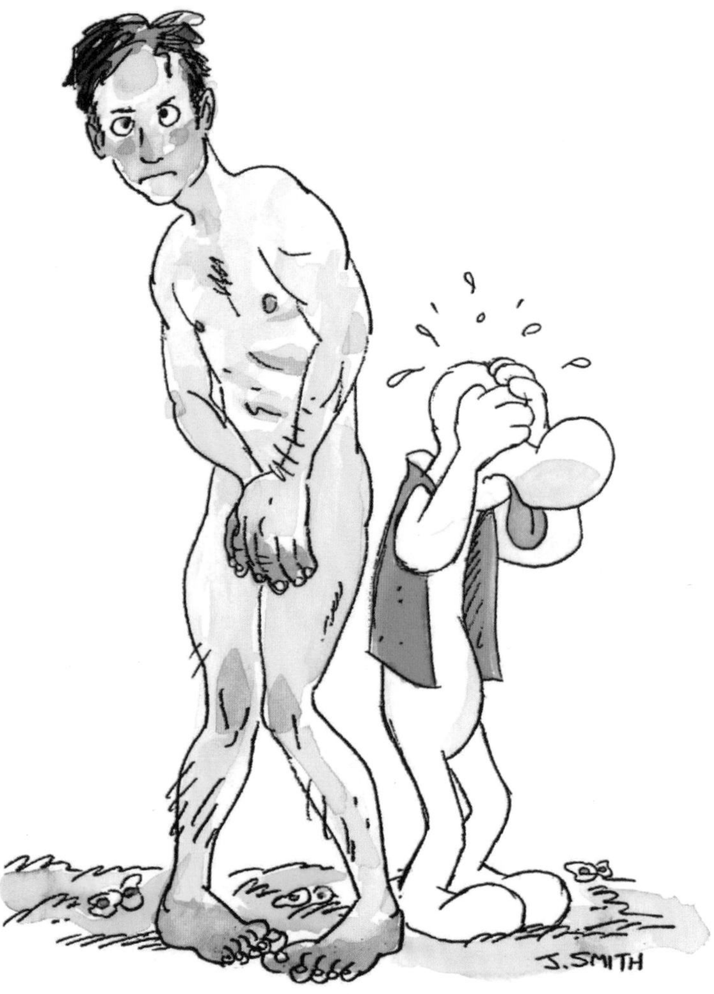
J. SMITH

JEFF AND HIS EMBARRASSED BONE.

Rob Smith Jr. (b. 1963, Orlando, FL) got his start in high school, drawing caricatures at theme parks and stands around Central Florida. He attended the Ringling School of Art, the Joe Kubert School of Cartoon and Graphic Art and Rollins College. In 1985, Jeff Parker (*Mother Goose and Grimm*) hired him as draftsman and artist for the City of Orlando, while he continued his caricature work for various tourist attractions, including Walt Disney World. Smith soon turned to editorial cartoons, drawing for the *Winter Park Observer* and *The Ledger*. He earned six Florida Press Association awards for his work and eventually landed a job drawing editorial cartoons for the *Glenn Beck Program*. Smith is a current member of the National Cartoonists Society and runs a cartoonist group in Tampa Bay called The Suncoast Inkslingers.

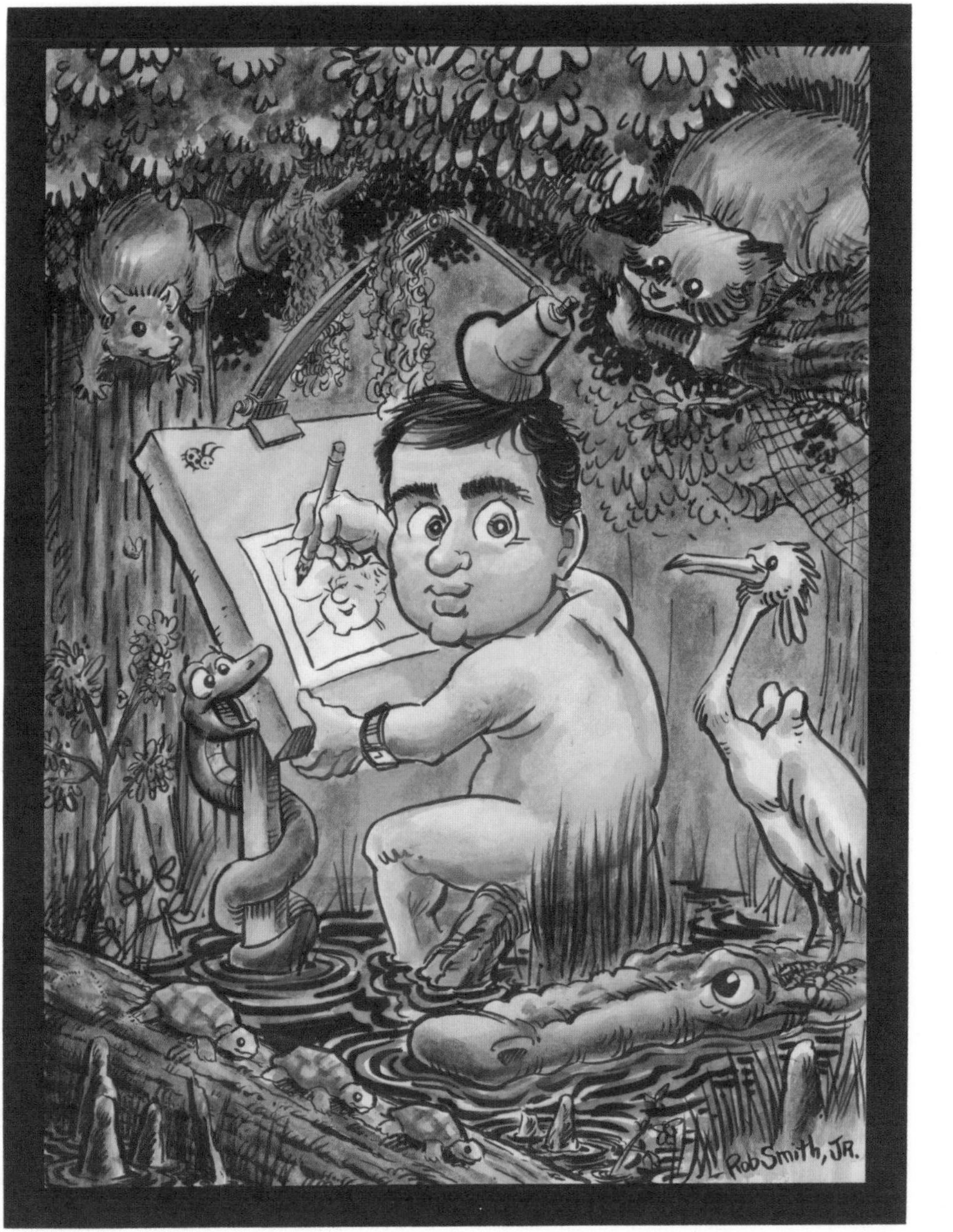
Rob Smith, JR.

Art Spiegelman (b. 1948, Stockholm, Sweden) immigrated to the United States in his early childhood with his parents, who were Polish Jews. Spiegelman grew up in Queens, NY, and studied at the High School of Art and Design in Manhattan. He majored in art and philosophy at Harpur College, but left school in 1968 to participate in the underground comics movement. He was a regular contributor to publications such as *Real Pulp*, *Young Lust* and *Bizarre Sex*. In 1975 he co-founded *Arcade* with Bill Griffith. In 1978 he married Françoise Mouly and in 1980 the couple started *Raw*, which serialized Spiegelman's *Maus*.

Maus was later collected into book form, for which Spiegelman won the Pulitzer Prize, an Eisner Award, and a Harvey Award in 1992. In the same year he was hired at *The New Yorker*, where he worked for 10 years. Spiegelman released *In the Shadow of No Towers* in 2004. He was named one of *Time*'s Top 100 Most Influential People in 2005. He was inducted into the Will Eisner Award Hall of Fame in 1999. Spiegelman and Mouly have a son and a daughter and live in New York City.

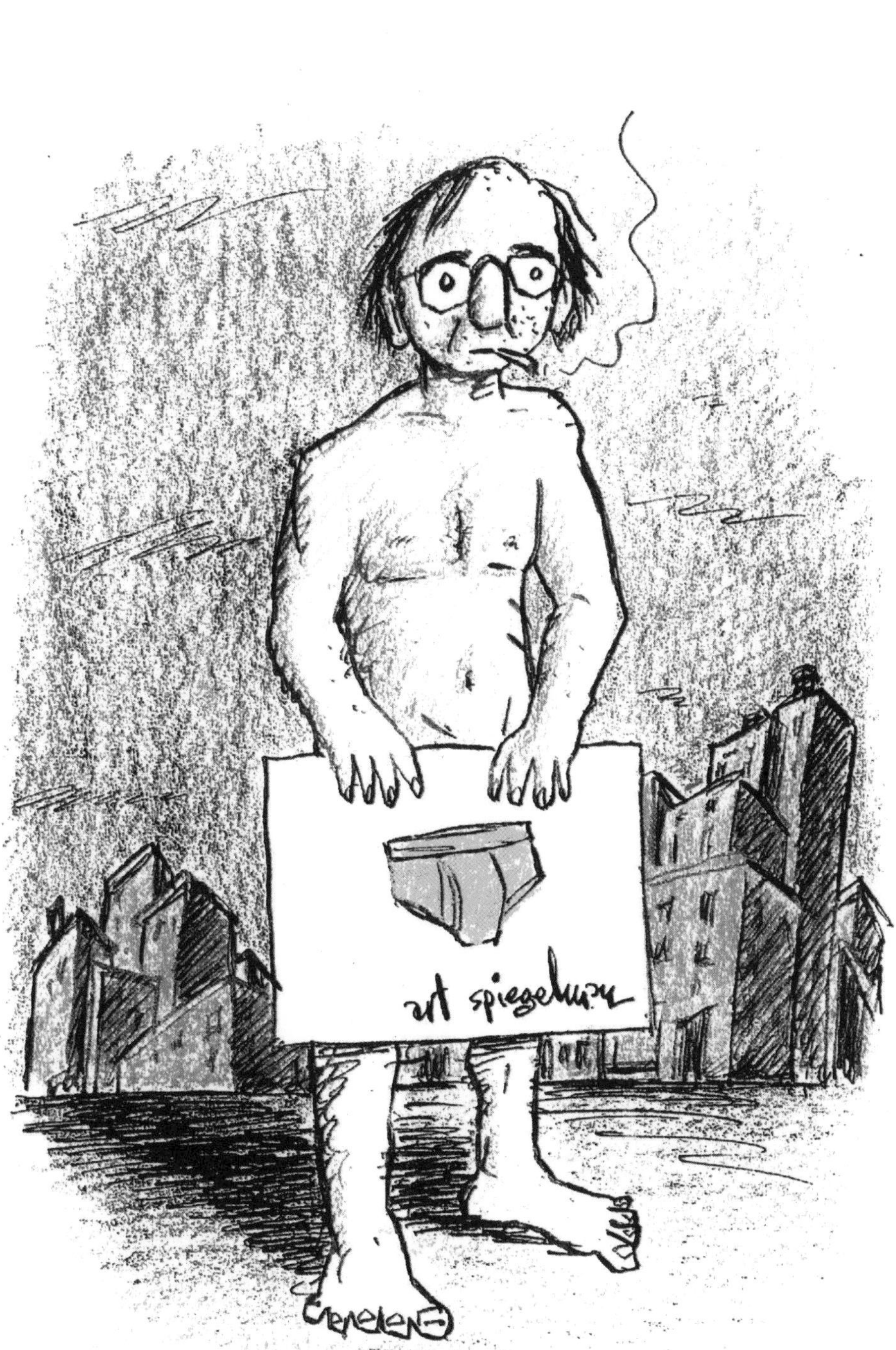
art spiegelman

Jeff Stahler (b. 1955), a native of Bellefontaine, OH, attended the Columbus College of Art and Design, graduating in 1977. He has been the editorial cartoonist for *The Columbus Citizen-Journal*, *The Cincinnati Post*, *The Columbus Dispatch* and his work has appeared in national newspapers such as *The New York Times* and *USA Today*. He also does the one-panel daily *Moderately Confused*. Winner of the 1990 John Fischetti Editorial Cartoon Competition as well as other cartooning awards. he and his family reside in Columbus, OH.

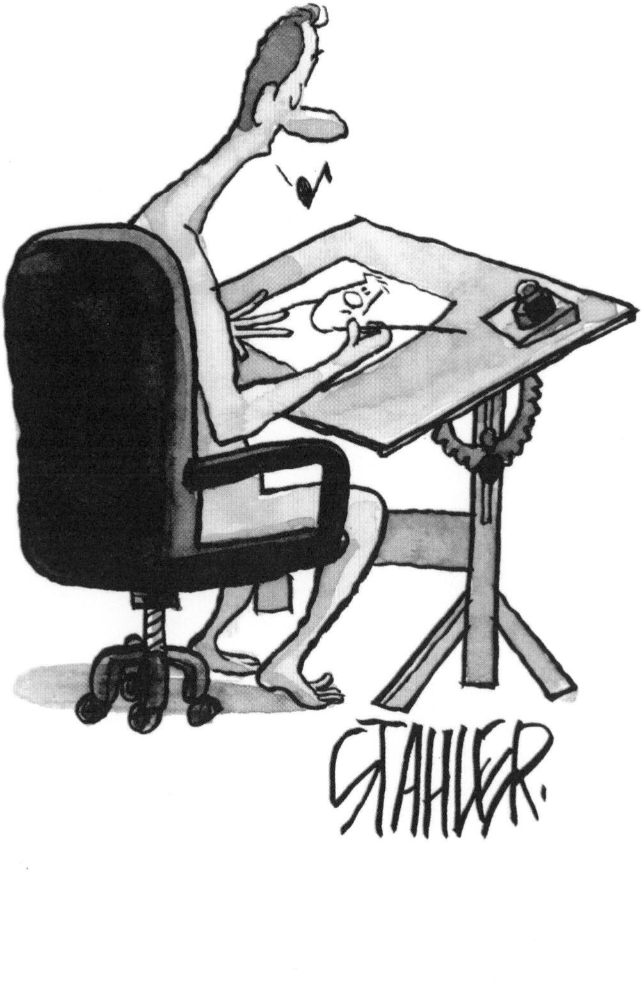
STAHLER.

Ann C. Telnaes (b. 1960, Stockholm, Sweden) studied character animation at California Institute of the Arts. She has worked on several animated Disney movies, including *The Brave Little Toaster*. Her editorial cartoons have been featured in *The New York Times*, *The Washington Post* and hundreds of other newspapers throughout the U.S. In 2001 she won the Pulitzer Prize for editorial cartooning. Telnaes lives in Washington, D.C. with her husband, David Lloyd.

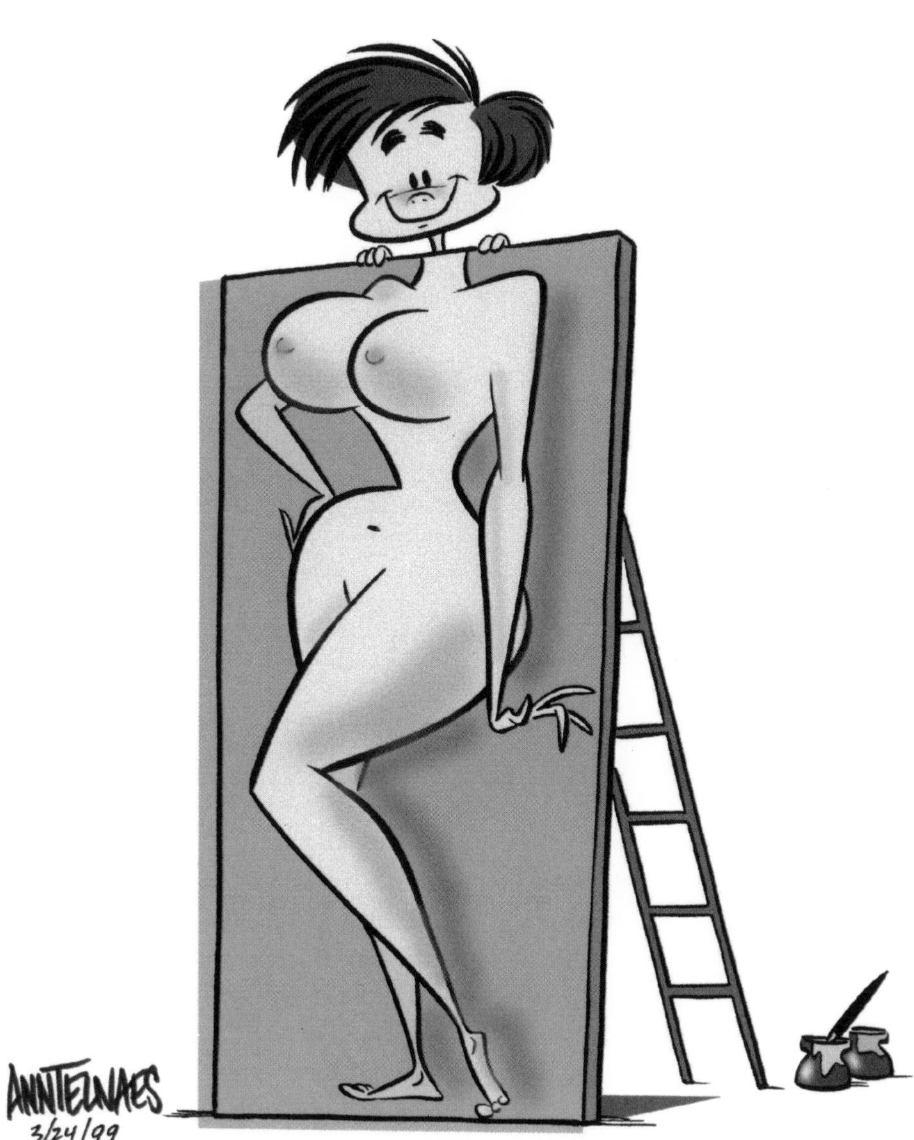
ANNTELNAES
3/24/99

Peaco Todd (b. Richmond, VA) earned a Master of Arts degree in Humanities from San Francisco State University in 1976. She started out as a copywriter who freelanced on the side, but she switched over to illustration after attending a greeting card workshop. Hallmark Cards hired her soon thereafter. A couple years later, Todd moved back to the East Coast, where she lived in Martha's Vineyard on a sailboat, painting names on boat hulls. She settled in Boston and taught for the Cambridge Center for Adult Education. She published *Porkbarrel Comix* in 2004 and 2008, works as a columnist for various newspapers around the region and does work for the annual Ig Nobel Award Ceremony.

Morrie Turner (b. 1923, Oakland, CA) joined the Army-Air Force after graduating from high school in 1942. He used his own war experiences to draw *Rail Head*, a series published by *Stars and Stripes*. After the war, he freelanced for various national publications while working for the Oakland Police Department. Noticing a lack of minorities in cartoons, he created the series *Wee Pals* (1965) — the first American cartoon to celebrate ethnic diversity. The result was huge success, earning the series publication in over 100 different newspapers worldwide. Turner went on to write a handful of children's books that included *The Prophet of Peace,* an illustrated biography of Martin Luther King, Jr. He received the "Sparky Award" in 2000 from the San Francisco Cartoon Art Museum. Morrie Turner currently lives in Sacramento, CA, where he still produces *Wee Pals.*

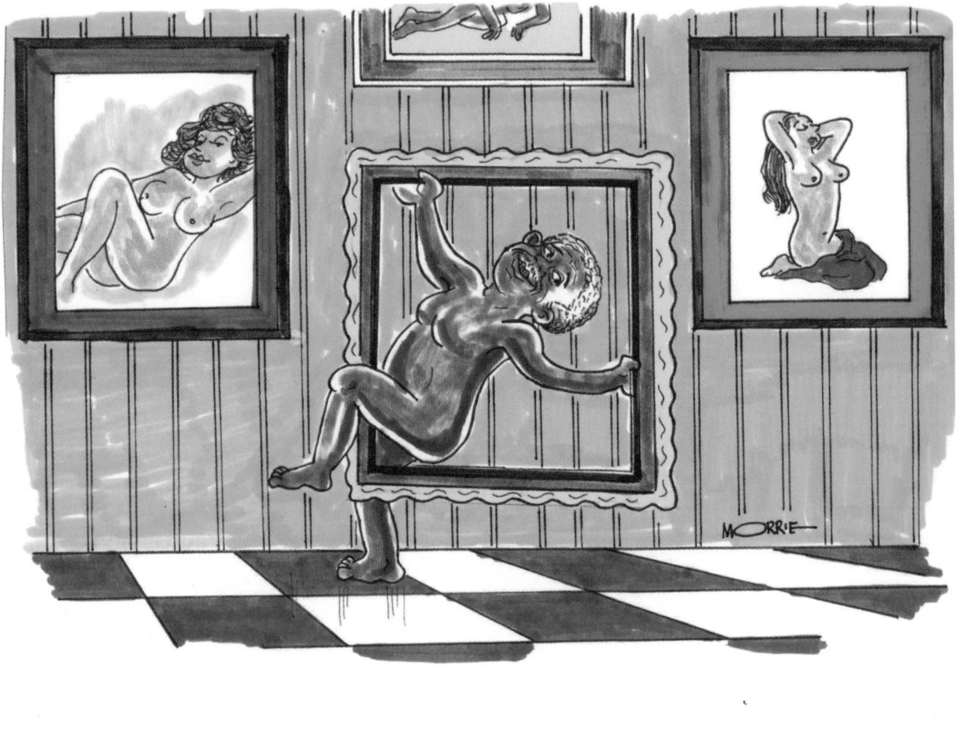
MORRIE

Mike Twohy (b. Palo Alto, CA) started his cartooning career at age 11 when he submitted his first comic to a newspaper. During high school Twohy worked on sports-related cartoons for the local paper and illustrated reading and math workbooks. In 1973, Twohy graduated from UC Berkeley where he received an M.F.A. in painting. After college, Twohy became a freelance cartoonist for periodicals such as *Esquire* and *TV Guide*. In 1980 Twohy began publishing his work in *The New Yorker*. His most well-known work is the one-panel comic strip *That's Life!* He and his wife live in Berkeley, CA.

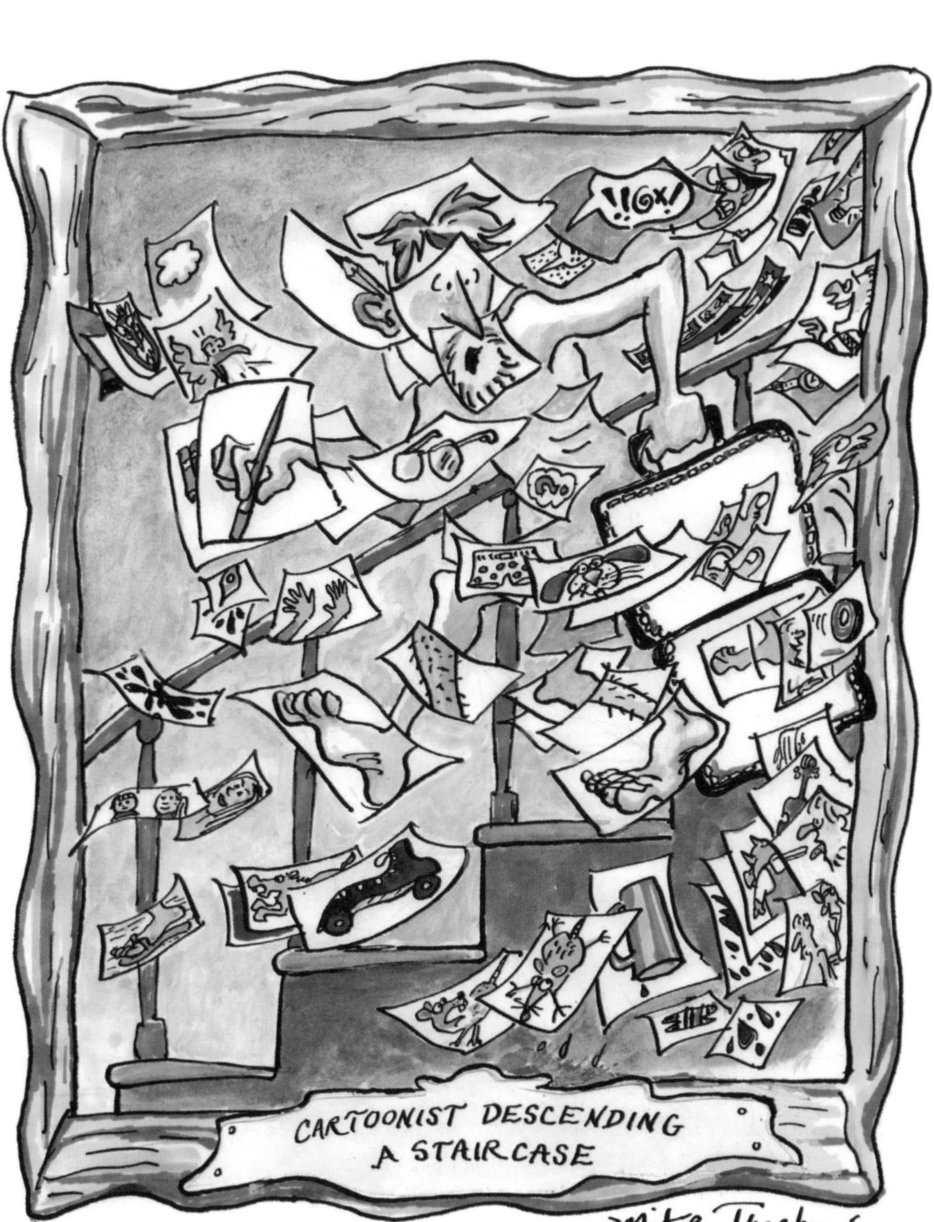
CARTOONIST DESCENDING
A STAIRCASE
Mike Twohy '99

Jerry Van Amerongen (b. 1940 in Grand Rapids, MI) attended the Ferris Institute in Michigan. At the age of 40 he began cartooning professionally. He has had two syndicated one-panel comics, *The Neighborhood* and *Ballard Street*. The latter won the National Cartoonists Society Newspaper Panel Award in 2004 and 2006. He works with Creators Syndicate and resides in Minneapolis, MN.

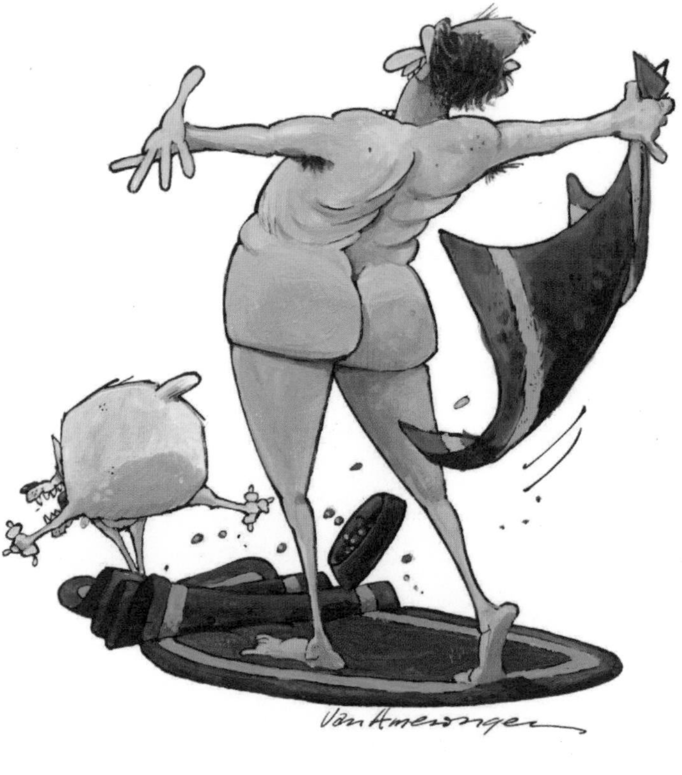
Van Amerongen

For Mark and Rosie, with lots of love – Jerry Van Amerongen

Mort Walker (b. 1923, El Dorado, KS) published his first cartoon at age 11, sold his first at 12 and by 14 was selling cartoons to *Child Life*, *Inside Detective* and *Flying Aces* magazines. He was a cartoonist for the *Kansas City Journal* as a teenager, and at 18 he had established himself as the chief editorial designer for Hall Bros., where he worked on Hallmark Cards. In 1943, Walker found himself in the Army, where he served as intelligence and investigating officer in Italy and was in charge of a German POW camp. After the war earned his bachelor's degree from the University of Missouri. During this time, he began drawing what would turn out to be his most popular strip: *Beetle Bailey*. Walker's work made its way into newspapers all across the country and eventually worldwide. The strip *Hi and Lois* spun off from *Beetle Bailey*, and Walker and his children continue to work on the strips to this day.

In 1974, Walker founded the Museum of Cartoon Art, the collection of which now resides at The Ohio State University Billy Ireland Cartoon Library & Museum. He has won the Reuben Award as well as many other newspaper-strip awards. He also received the American Legion's Fourth Estate Award in 1978. In 2000, the United States Army bestowed on him the Decoration for Distinguished Civilian Service.

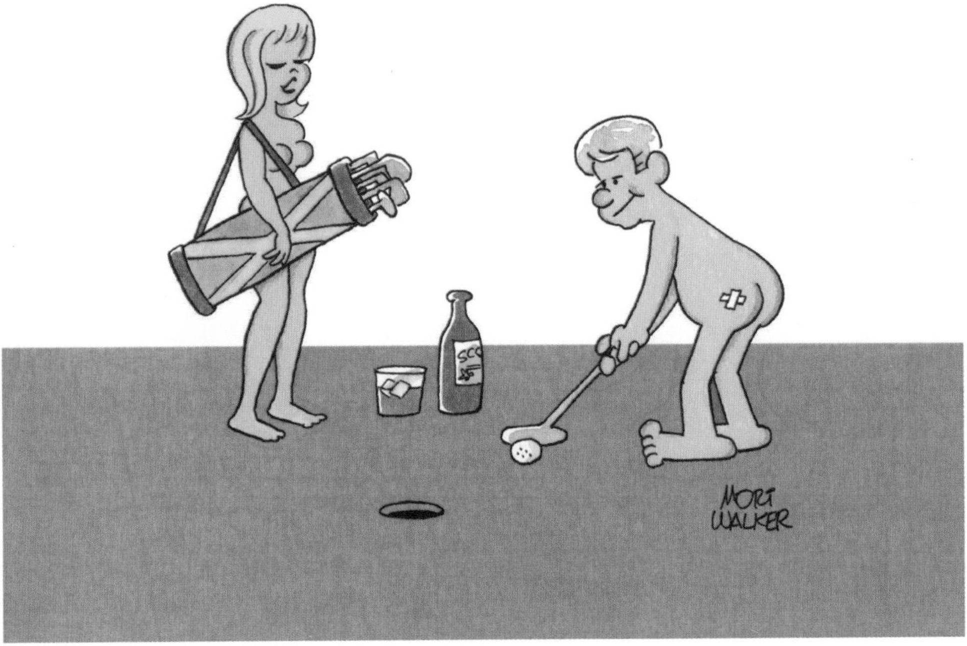
SCO
MORT WALKER

Gahan Wilson (b. 1930, Evanston, IL)'s horror-fantasy cartoons and prose writings have been featured regularly in *Playboy* and *The New Yorker* for more than 50 years. Wilson is also known for his many children's stories, including *Harry, the Fat Spy Bear* (1973) and *Spooky Stories for a Dark and Stormy Night* (1994). Wilson's strip *Nuts* ran in *National Lampoon* in the 1970s and '80s and has recently been compiled into a single volume. Wilson was recognized with a World Fantasy Convention Award in 1981, and in 2005 he received both a Lifetime Achievement Award from the World Fantasy Awards and a Milton Caniff Lifetime Achievement Award from the National Cartoonists Society.

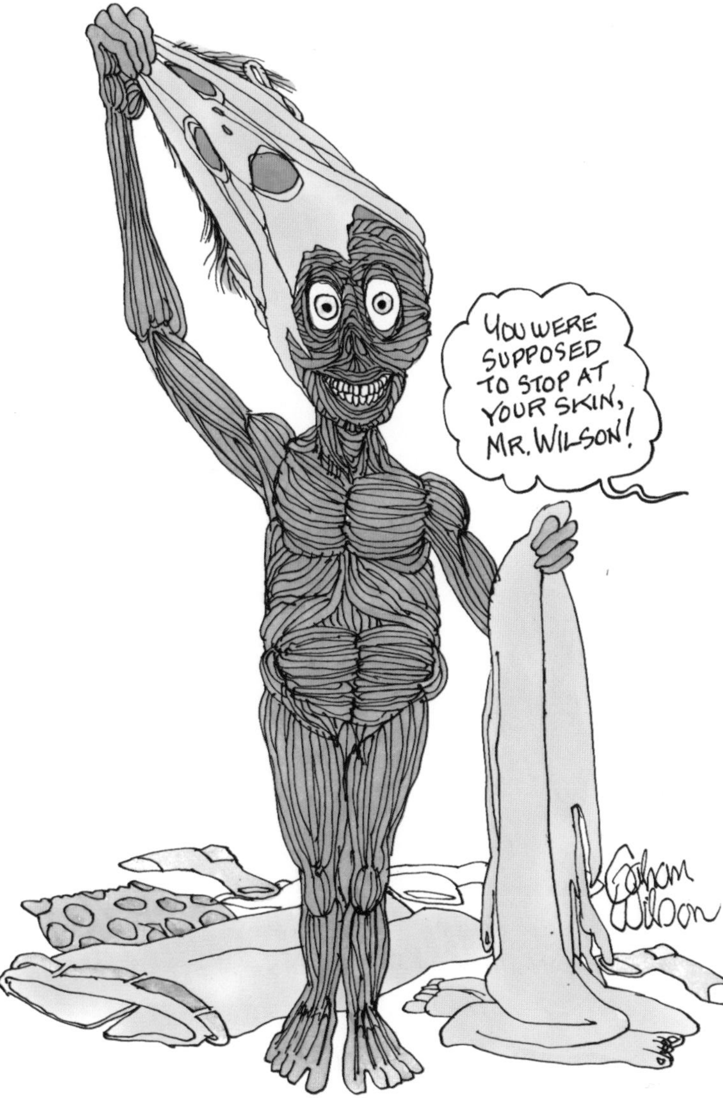
YOU WERE SUPPOSED TO STOP AT YOUR SKIN, MR. WILSON!
Gahan Wilson